THE GRAND AMERICAN ODESSEY

90 Days Across America and Beyond

JN370162

Dr. Narayan Pratap
Veterinarian and Traveller

THE GRAND AMERICAN ODYSSEY

90 Days Across America and Beyond

By

Dr. Narayan Pratap

A journey across landscapes, memories, and the heart.

Bangalore, India - 2025

Clever Fox® PUBLISHING

Chennai • Bangalore

CLEVER FOX PUBLISHING
Chennai, India

Published by CLEVER FOX PUBLISHING 2026
Copyright © Dr. Narayan Pratap 2026

All Rights Reserved.
ISBN: 978-93-7500-199-7

This book has been published with all reasonable efforts taken to make the material error-free after the consent of the author. No part of this book shall be used, reproduced in any manner whatsoever without written permission from the author, except in the case of brief quotations embodied in critical articles and reviews.

The Author of this book is solely responsible and liable for its content including but not limited to the views, representations, descriptions, statements, information, opinions and references ["Content"]. The Content of this book shall not constitute or be construed or deemed to reflect the opinion or expression of the Publisher or Editor. Neither the Publisher nor Editor endorse or approve the Content of this book or guarantee the reliability, accuracy or completeness of the Content published herein and do not make any representations or warranties of any kind, express or implied, including but not limited to the implied warranties of merchantability, fitness for a particular purpose. The Publisher and Editor shall not be liable whatsoever for any errors, omissions, whether such errors or omissions result from negligence, accident, or any other cause or claims for loss or damages of any kind, including without limitation, indirect or consequential loss or damage arising out of use, inability to use, or about the reliability, accuracy or sufficiency of the information contained in this book.

Dedication

This book is dedicated to my father, **late Narayan**, *and my mother,* **Sudha**, *who brought us up and are the reason for what we are today.*

To my elder brother, **Surya Prakash**, *an inspiration, and a gifted author whose published eBooks have motivated me.*

To my sisters, **Prabha** *and* **Priya**, *and my loving younger brother,* **Srinivas Manohar**, *for their constant warmth and encouragement.*

And to my wonderful wife, **Sunitha**, *my partner in every adventure;*

our adorable daughter **Neha**, *and our awesome son-in-law* **Abhishek**, *whose love fills every journey with joy and meaning.*

EPIGRAPH

"The world reveals its best secrets to those who walk its roads with wonder in their hearts."

– Dr. Narayan Pratap

CONTENTS

PREFACE

"Journeys end, but their echoes stay with us, in every sunrise, every smile, and every story we remember."

– Narayan Pratap

After decades of service as a veterinarian, my lifelong curiosity to explore the world finally carried me onto an extraordinary adventure: an unforgettable ninety-day odyssey across the United States and beyond. Travel, to me, has always been more than movement; it is discovery, connection, and the quiet rediscovery of oneself through new eyes. This travelogue is not merely a record of destinations, but a tapestry of experiences: the people we met, the cultures we encountered, the landscapes that humbled us, and the small, delightful moments that shaped each day of our journey.

In the summer of 2025, my wife, Sunitha, and I embarked on a once-in-a-lifetime voyage, beginning with a long flight from Bengaluru to New York City. The joy of being reunited with our daughter, Neha, and son-in-law, Abhishek, set the tone for everything that followed. Our early days unfolded gently: shared meals, unhurried conversations, and explorations of quiet towns and scenic corners that made us feel instantly at home. Soon, the energy and diversity of New York City drew us in, and we found ourselves wandering through its many neighbourhoods, each alive with its own rhythm and character.

From there, our journey widened into a coast-to-coast exploration that carried us through historic cities, iconic landmarks, and breathtaking natural wonders. We experienced places steeped in history, others bursting with modern excitement, and landscapes so vast and silent that they demanded humility. Each stop offered something unique: moments of awe, joy, reflection, and learning, woven together into a journey far richer than we had imagined.

As if the land itself were not enough, the sea beckoned next. A seven-day cruise carried us across turquoise waters to sun-washed islands, where endless horizons and the gentle rhythm of the ocean offered a serenity that still lingers in memory. Along the way, our travels also became a journey of reunion and reconnection, as we spent cherished time with relatives and friends across different cities. A peaceful retreat into nature followed, where rocky shores, quiet forests, and star-filled skies reminded us of the world's timeless beauty. Witnessing the Fourth of July fireworks, surrounded by thousands celebrating with pride and joy, remains one of the most unforgettable moments of our stay.

Over ninety remarkable days, we crossed cities, oceans, landscapes, and milestones. This book is a humble record of those moments: a travelogue of gratitude, wonder, and shared joy, written in the hope that it may inspire others to step out, embrace curiosity, and allow the world to unfold its magic before them.

INTRODUCTION

"Travel is the quiet teacher that shows us how vast the world is; and how much of ourselves we have yet to discover."

This travelogue recounts our memorable journey to the United States of America: a dream destination since our childhood, not only for us but for countless people across India and around the world. That dream finally became a reality through the grace of God and the blessings of our parents, family, and well-wishers. What once felt like a distant wish slowly unfolded into one of the most unforgettable chapters of our lives.

The planning and preparation for this journey began nearly eighteen months in advance. At the time, the waiting period for a *United States visitor visa* in India stretched to almost three years. With timely support from the Indian Ministry of External Affairs, the wait was reduced to about a year and a half. During this period, our daughter, Neha, and son-in-law, Abhishek, stepped in to guide us with immense care and patience.

With their help, we were able to complete every formal step smoothly, from filling out the DS-160 non-immigrant visa form to scheduling the two appointments at the *United States Consulate General, Chennai.* The first visit passed quickly with document verification and fingerprinting. The second: the main visa interview, was the moment that truly mattered. We still remember the joy in our hearts when the pleasant consular officer smiled warmly and said, *"Congratulations, both your visas have been approved. Welcome to the United States!"* From that moment onward, our excitement knew no bounds.

Soon after, we coordinated our travel dates with Neha and Abhishek and booked our flights. Our journey was finalized for the last week of April, flying from Bengaluru to New York via London Heathrow. Our return was scheduled for the final weekend of the third week of July, departing from JFK Airport via Amsterdam Schiphol and returning to Bengaluru.

To make the most of our stay, we also booked an eighteen-day all-inclusive East and West Coast tour with Chariot Travels, Bengaluru. Neha and Abhishek went a step further and arranged a seven-day cruise to the Bahamas from New York: yet another dream come true. Their meticulous planning and involvement made us feel supported, cherished, and deeply grateful.

With hearts full of anticipation, gratitude, and love, we eagerly awaited the day our American adventure would begin. Little did we know that the ninety days ahead would become one of the most enriching and joyful journeys of our lives, made all the more meaningful because it was shared in the wonderful company of our daughter and son-in-law.

THE JOURNEY BEGINS:

DECISION AND DEPARTURE

CHAPTER 1

THE JOURNEY BEGINS: DECISION AND DEPARTURE

"Every journey begins long before the first step; in the quiet hope that life has more wonders to show us."

Ours began with a calendar and a dream that refused to stay quiet. For months, a pencilled note sat on the corner of my study table: *"90 Days - USA."* It had started as a half-serious thought after my wife, Sunitha, and I missed a family trip to the United States in 2016 because of my work schedule.

The idea grew stronger after our darling daughter, Neha, got married and moved to Jersey City with our son-in-law, Abhishek. The next step was clear: to apply for and obtain a visitor visa to the United States.

Eventually, that distant idea turned into reality, complete with an itinerary too full for a single page: temples, museums, waterfalls, a cruise, and countless miles of American road. We were especially blessed that our daughter travelled to India for her visa renewal and could accompany us on our journey to the United States, a comforting thought indeed.

On a warm April morning in Bengaluru, we zipped our suitcases, bidding a temporary goodbye to our parents and family. We took one last look at the house that had been alive with planning for weeks. Documents were triple-checked, chargers packed, and snacks tucked into every spare pocket.

There is a distinct kind of calm that comes just before a long journey: the silence of finality before movement begins. The cab ride to the airport felt unusually quiet, the roads stretching ahead like an invitation.

At *Kempe Gowda International Airport*, the lines were mercifully short, the air heavy with the mixed scent of coffee and jet fuel. As we waited to board our flight to London Heathrow, time slowed into a series of small, comforting details: boarding passes with their precise fonts, the hum of luggage belts, the quick farewell calls that always end with *"Take care."* "Travel, I realised, is made more of these small rituals than of grand destinations.

After months of planning, the day had finally arrived. We set out on our long-awaited journey from Bengaluru, excitement palpable. The engine hummed like a sleeping city as we taxied past the runway lights.

Ninety days had been pinned onto the travel calendar in a few impulsive strokes of colour: a festival of pins that back home had felt like the kind of dream you scroll past and forget. But here we were, passports in hand and heads full of lists, the plan loose yet wonderfully specific.

Leaving Bengaluru at dawn, the sky held the thin, hopeful light of a page not yet written. The nine-hour flight to Heathrow passed in the suspended half-sleep of long travel. Through the oval window, the curve of the earth wore a thin shawl of light.

A young attendant with a crisp accent offered tea, and somewhere between sips I began sketching in my notebook: *Heathrow - JFK - New Jersey.* That was the first moment the trip felt real.

Transit at Heathrow

London greeted us with its familiar drizzle. *Heathrow's Terminal 5* was a hive of polite chaos, languages colliding in soft bursts, duty-free counters glowing like shrines to temptation. The layover stretched long enough for reflection. I watched aircraft lift off one after another and wondered about all the beginnings contained within those flights.

Somewhere between a cup of hot chocolate and a walk through an endless glass corridor, fatigue folded itself into excitement. In those neutral hours of waiting, we were neither here nor there: suspended travellers between continents. When our connecting flight was called, we walked toward the gate with the quiet certainty of people stepping into a new chapter.

Arrival in New York

The long flight across continents culminated in a thrilling descent over New York City, the skyline glittering under a crisp morning sun, the Statue of Liberty welcoming us with her timeless grace. After nearly twenty hours in transit, the first sight of New York felt like stepping into a movie we already knew by heart.

At *JFK Airport*, formalities were smooth, and the moment we stepped outside, a wave of realization hit: we were truly in America. Immigration lines were long but efficient, and the officer was courteous. When he stamped our passports with a mechanical thud, that single sound: ink on paper, felt like an arrival far deeper than geography.

Outside, the cool April wind cut through our travel-warmed clothes. New York's air smelled of asphalt, coffee, and promise. Abhishek was waiting in the parking lot, and Neha's call guided him to the exit. The joy of seeing each other after so long was overwhelming.

The GPS screen blinked awake, and a calm American voice began directing us toward *Jersey City, New Jersey*: our home base for the next three months. As the city receded behind us, bridges arched over rivers like gateways to new beginnings, while Neha and Abhishek pointed out sights along the way.

It felt like bliss, almost dreamlike. Yet the real arrival was not just the city that greeted us, but the rhythm we soon found in New Jersey: small pockets of calm tucked between highways, weekday commutes giving way to quieter rituals.

We finally reached home sweet home. The first evening ended not with fanfare, but with silence: the satisfying stillness after too much motion. Abhishek and Neha treated us to a lovely homemade dinner, and we slept early, lulled by the hum of the heater and the distant sounds of passing vehicles, ambulances, and fire trucks.

NEW JERSEY: THE LAUNCHPAD

EVERY ADVENTURE NEEDS A BEGINNING: OURS BEGAN HERE IN THE GARDEN STATE

CHAPTER 2

NEW JERSEY: THE LAUNCHPAD

"To know a place, walk its quiet corners; they reveal more than any map ever will."

Every long journey needs a quiet beginning: a place where one can settle, stretch, and begin to listen to a new country breathe. For us, that place was *New Jersey*, a state often mistaken for *New York City's* quieter cousin, yet one that revealed itself, day by day, as a tapestry of stillness, ritual, and discovery.

Settling into the Rhythm

Every morning began with a faint chill, the kind that makes coffee taste stronger. The neighbourhood awoke slowly: a school bus sighing to a halt, joggers with earbuds weaving through the fog, the rhythmic creak of someone's sprinkler.

The first few days were devoted to settling in: learning the scale of American grocery stores, figuring out why milk came in gallons and bread in endless varieties, and adjusting to the mysterious American thermostat that always seemed too cold or too warm. Before long, curiosity nudged us beyond domestic details and onto the road.

The days unfolded gently. Jet lag woke us before dawn, so mornings began with misty walks along empty sidewalks. In those quiet hours, the neighbourhood felt like a film set waiting for its actors.

The Temple That Felt Like Home

Our first weekend took us to the *Bridgewater Balaji Temple*, set amid tree-lined streets that whispered of suburban calm. The two-hour drive from Jersey City felt almost meditative: wide roads bordered by flowering dogwoods, Maple and Oak trees, the radio offering a gentle mix of Indian melodies and local advertisements.

As we approached, a golden *gopuram* rose above the treeline, its intricate carvings catching the sunlight with quiet dignity. Stepping inside felt like walking into a piece of home carried lovingly across oceans. The familiar rhythm of Sanskrit chants filled the halls as priests moved gracefully between rituals, their voices steady and serene. The fragrance of sandalwood, jasmine, and ghee lamps dissolved whatever remained of our jet lag.

In that moment, we were no longer travellers; we were participants. Bells chimed softly, incense smoke curled toward carved ceilings, and outside, tulips swayed in the cool wind. Indian families moved through the space, children dressed in traditional attire, their laughter echoing gently through the complex. We later enjoyed a delicious lunch at the spacious restaurant within the temple grounds.

That evening, back home, we went up to the terrace on the tenth floor to watch the *New York skyline*. The rain had just passed, and as the sun dipped lower, the city took on a warm golden glow. Just as Neha had predicted, a rainbow appeared: softly arcing against the skyline, an unexpected and perfect ending to one of our first days in America.

Blossoms and Beginnings

By mid-April, *Essex County's Branch Brook Park* had turned into a pastel dreamscape. Spring in parts of the United States, especially New Jersey, carries a subtle beauty in the form of cherry blossoms. At their peak, thousands of delicate pink blooms fluttered in the breeze.

We drove out early from *Jersey City to Newark*, arriving well before the crowds. Soon we were walking beneath canopies that felt like painted clouds. Petals drifted down like snowflakes, settling on benches, car roofs, and even the edges of our camera lenses. Every photograph looked surreal, as though the world's saturation had been gently turned up. Couples posed for portraits, children chased falling blossoms, and a lone violinist beneath a tree played soft notes that scattered into the wind.

Standing amid such fragile beauty, I thought of time: how it races through airports yet slows in gardens. Spring was not merely a season; it was a conversation between endings and beginnings. Fragile and pink against grey skies, like watercolour in motion, it felt like pure bliss to be there among the cherry blossoms. We felt especially fortunate, knowing they bloom for only a brief few weeks between March and April.

Evenings were often spent on short drives, learning which highways merged into which, tasting the geography through movement. We also walked frequently to *Lincoln Park*, a vast and lively green space close to our home. Shaded by towering trees and always alive with activity, the park drew people of all ages: children and adults playing football, baseball, basketball, cricket, tennis, and pickleball; others cycling or strolling along the tracks; families gathering near the lake with its graceful fountains.

Being so close to Newark Airport, we often watched planes take off and land during our walks. Ambulances and patrol cars passed by regularly, and the cheerful jingle of an ice-cream truck playing *"Jingle Bells"* became a familiar soundtrack to our evenings.

Among the most cherished memories of our stay were these frequent visits to Lincoln Park in Jersey City. Just a two-kilometre walk from Neha's home, the park felt like a living, breathing world of its own: well laid out, safe, and welcoming, with clean roads marked at 25 mph, ample parking, and a strong sense of community woven into everyday life.

My long walks there became a personal sanctuary. I often completed two full rounds: nearly ten kilometres including the walk to and from Neha's place. Sunsets glowed behind planes lifting off from Newark Airport, fountains shimmered across the ponds, and once, I even captured a perfect full moon on my phone.

At night, the four of us would sit together scrolling through maps and making lists for the weeks ahead: a Manhattan food tour,

Macy's, Staten Island, SoJo Spa, a shooting range, Pennsylvania waterfalls, relatives in Chicago, and the long East–West loop that awaited us. The list kept growing, and so did our excitement.

The Mountain and the River

A week later, drawn by a longing for open skies and fresh mountain air, we set out for *Bear Mountain*, which rises along the border of Rockland and Orange Counties in New York State.

The road wound through forests so green they seemed to hum. In the distance, the Hudson River gleamed, and every few miles a sign pointed toward a viewpoint promising a *"Scenic Overlook."*

The climb was moderate, but the reward immense. From the summit, we watched the river curl like a silver ribbon far below, tiny boats tracing slow lines across its surface. The wind carried the scent of pine and distant rain. We unpacked our sandwiches and soft drinks and, for a long while, did nothing more than watch the clouds change shape.

Travel often teaches through contrast. After the dense human energy of New York City and Jersey City, the silence of Bear Mountain felt almost sacred.

Bear Mountain State Park, a popular day trip from both New Jersey and New York City, offered a perfect balance of nature, history, and recreation: wide views, wooded trails, and the rare thrill of finding such stillness so close to a metropolis.

The park takes its name from the mountain itself, said to resemble a *sleeping bear*. We walked a portion of the *Appalachian*

Trail that loops for about three miles around Hessian Lake, then descended a long flight of steps to the pier at the Hudson's edge. A train thundered past on a nearby bridge, while anglers stood patiently along the water, trying their luck.

On the drive back, we stopped at a small roadside cafe. The owner, an elderly man wearing a New York Yankees cap, asked, *"You folks visiting?"* We nodded. He smiled and said, *"Good. There's more America out here than in Times Square."* I wrote that line down. He was right.

Cider and Simplicity

A few days later, our journey led us to a place simple in essence yet unforgettable in spirit: *Red Barn Cidery*, set on the historic grounds of Dr. Davies Farm in Congers, New York. Rows of apple trees stretched across gentle slopes, their leaves trembling softly in the breeze.

We arrived on a quiet weekday afternoon, when the crowds were thin and a farm dog lazed near the entrance. Inside the rustic barn shop, shelves were lined with cider bottles, jars of honey, and apple pies so fragrant they seemed to glow.

Abhishek and Neha introduced us to cider so crisp it felt like sunlight captured in liquid form. The tasting flight arrived on a wooden tray, each glass glowing in shades of amber and gold. We sampled *classic dry, semi-dry, sweet, fruited, spiced, and sparkling* varieties. The aromas unfolded gently: freshly cut apples, lemon zest, honey, faint caramel, cranberry, cinnamon, and clove.

Each sip told the story of the orchard, from the crisp air of the Hudson Valley to the patient hands that had tended these trees for generations. The ciders differed in personality, yet all shared the same spirit: fresh, honest, and deeply local. The farm is also known for its apple-picking season, which draws visitors from August through November.

As we lingered over our tasting: golden, crisp, and faintly tart; we chatted with the woman behind the counter. She told us the farm had remained family-run since the 1890s. *"Each tree here,"* she said with a smile, *"is older than your passports."* We left with two bottles of cider and a gentle lesson in simplicity.

There is something grounding about places where life still revolves around soil, sunlight, and patience. On the drive back, the car carried the faint scent of apples and open fields. With each outing, our surroundings felt less like a destination and more like a place we were beginning to belong to.

Mother's Day Celebration

We were truly fortunate to be with our daughter, Neha, during the Mother's Day celebrations. She and Abhishek treated us to a lovely *Mother's Day brunch at the Rooftop Exchange Place* in New Jersey.

It was a memorable experience filled with warmth, elegance, and togetherness. Perched high above the Hudson River, the rooftop offered sweeping views of the Manhattan skyline: an ideal backdrop to celebrate a mother's love and grace.

The air was cool, and the sky carried a soft spring glow. Families filled the terrace, their cheerful conversations rising gently above the music. From that height, Manhattan appeared less like a city and more like a living sculpture, each window glowing, each bridge catching the light.

As we arrived, a light breeze carried with it a sense of joy and gratitude. The glass-walled terrace glowed with afternoon light, and the atmosphere felt festive yet intimate. A beautifully arranged brunch buffet awaited us, with fresh pastries, colourful salads, thoughtfully prepared dishes, and desserts that looked as if they belonged in an art gallery. The staff welcomed each guest with warm smiles and roses, making every mother and mother-to-be feel truly special.

As we dined and laughed together, the skyline sparkled across the river. Sunitha's eyes lit up with happiness as we raised a toast to her love and strength with sparkling mimosas. Music, laughter, and soft conversations blended into a gentle rhythm of celebration.

Later, as the light softened, we captured a few family photographs against the breathtaking view: timeless reminders of a day filled with gratitude and love. Celebrating Mother's Day at the Rooftop Exchange Place was more than a meal; it was an emotional experience, a tribute to motherhood, and a moment of deep connection that will stay with me forever.

After brunch, we walked along the Hudson Riverfront, spending a peaceful hour watching geese and seagulls glide across the water while sailboats drifted past. That evening became a quiet bookmark in our memory: the golden midpoint of our first month in America. As night settled in, we toasted to journeys, to mothers, and to distances made smaller by love.

Hoboken: Small Town with a Skyline

Our visit to *Hoboken*, New Jersey, was a delightful blend of charm, history, and breathtaking views. We travelled by bus from home, the hour-long ride offering lovely glimpses of Jersey Heights and the skyline as we descended toward the Hoboken pier.

Stepping off near the ferry terminal, the view before us was instantly captivating. Hoboken revealed itself with an easy small-town charm: rows of brownstone houses, cosy cafes, and locals who greeted one another with familiar nods.

At a riverside cafe, we ordered cappuccinos and cannoli, the kind of indulgence travel excuses. A guitarist played old Sinatra tunes; *"He was born here,"* the waiter reminded us with pride.

We wandered past the old clock tower and statues tinged green by time, well-preserved echoes of the city's past. Lawns and gardens opened toward a small park by the river, where the Hudson flowed steadily and the daytime skyline of downtown and midtown Manhattan stretched across the horizon. We also paused before the statue often referred to as the *Silent Lady*, standing calmly against the river breeze.

Just across the Hudson from Manhattan, Hoboken offered a refreshing contrast to the city's relentless pace. As we strolled along the scenic waterfront promenade, the skyline unfolded before us like a moving mural: perfect backdrop for photographs and quiet reflection. Cobblestone streets, historic buildings, and a lively yet relaxed atmosphere made each corner feel both quaint and cosmopolitan.

We passed the Hoboken Historical Museum, which offers glimpses into the city's rich past, and later walked by the historic *Stevens Institute of Technology,* founded in 1870, its campus overlooking the river with quiet academic grace. We lingered until sunset, watching the skyline change colour: from gold to rose to deep indigo. It was impossible not to fall a little in love with that view.

Hoboken's culinary scene was equally memorable, from cosy cafes serving artisanal coffee to waterfront restaurants offering seafood with spectacular city views. We enjoyed dinner at *Mamoun's Falafel* and later treated ourselves to dessert at *Rita's*, a famous Italian ice and frozen custard shop, sampling a variety of flavours.

The city's youthful energy, music, and welcoming spirit made it a place where tradition and modern life coexist beautifully. Our short visit to Hoboken turned out to be peaceful yet inspiring, leaving us with fond memories of New Jersey's hidden gem by the river.

A Spiritual Pause and Countryside Experiences in New Jersey

The *Swaminarayan Akshardham Temple* in Robbinsville, New Jersey, offered a spiritual experience that was both serene and awe-inspiring. Leaving from Jersey City, we drove for nearly two hours in our *Polestar 2, an electric vehicle*, to reach the temple tucked away in the quieter southern part of the state.

The temple's exterior was graced by a majestic 49-foot-tall statue of Bhagwan Swaminarayan, depicted as Nilkanth Varni: his youthful ascetic form when he left home at the age of eleven to embark on a life of spiritual seeking. His journey took him from the foothills of the Himalayas across vast stretches of India, covering more than 3,000 kilometres over four years, spreading spirituality and uplifting people wherever he went.

As we approached the grand white marble structure, its intricate carvings and serene presence stood out against the calm suburban surroundings. The temple's architecture felt like a true masterpiece: every pillar, dome, and sculpture reflecting devotion, artistry, and spiritual grace. Inside, the stillness was profound. Walking through the mandir complex, we admired the tranquil gardens and beautifully maintained pathways, where visitors moved with quiet reverence.

The harmony of art, faith, and silence made the visit deeply moving: a reminder that spirituality can be both majestic and simple, a divine experience nestled unexpectedly in the heart of New Jersey. After spending a few peaceful hours there, we concluded our visit with a meal at the on-site restaurant, which served authentic *sattvic Gujarati food*, nourishing both body and soul.

Countryside Experiences

From the temple, our journey continued into the countryside. We crossed the *Delaware River*, which separates New Jersey from Pennsylvania, and drove toward *Johnson's Corner Farm* in Medford, New Jersey: a charming strawberry-picking farm tucked deep amid open fields.

The transition was striking, from marble grandeur to wide green landscapes lined with rows of bright red strawberries glistening under the sun. The farm buzzed with cheerful activity: children enjoying hayrides, families picking seasonal fruits, and the inviting aroma of fresh pies and apple cider drifting from the country store.

We wandered through the farm market, browsing shelves stocked with homemade jams, baked goods, and local produce: each item carrying the comforting touch of farm freshness. After buying tickets for *strawberry picking*, we climbed onto a hay tractor trailer that took us out to the fields, a fun ride. With baskets in hand, we walked between the rows, plucking juicy strawberries straight from the plants.

The sweet fragrance in the air and the joy of picking our own fruit made the experience both refreshing and heartwarming.

The sweet fragrance in the air and the simple joy of picking our own fruit made the experience both refreshing and heartwarming. It felt like the perfect counterpoint to the temple's serene calm: a day that blended spirituality, nature, and the uncomplicated pleasures of rural life.

We returned with two boxes of strawberries, paying for what we picked. That very night, Neha delighted us with homemade strawberry ice cream prepared from our harvest, along with bowls of fresh strawberries: truly delicious and deeply satisfying.

Later, we stopped at an EV charging station beside a tranquil pond. To our delight, a couple of deer wandered past, unhurried and graceful. In that quiet moment, a deep sense of contentment washed over me, once again reminding me of the gentle joys that make rural New Jersey so memorable.

On our drive back home, Neha and Abhishek treated us to dinner at the famous Italian restaurant *Olive Garden*. Hot soup, unlimited house salad, creamy fettuccine Alfredo with broccoli, and an endless supply of breadsticks and sauces made for a hearty and joyful meal. The food was wonderful, the service warm, and the day ended on a note of comfort and gratitude.

An Exciting Shooting Experience: Guns for Hire, New Jersey

One unusual outing took us to *Guns for Hire*, a professional shooting range in Woodland Park, New Jersey. It was a completely different kind of thrill: one defined not by speed or spectacle, but by focus, discipline, and controlled excitement.

Abhishek and Neha introduced us to this well-organised facility, where we first registered and signed the required paperwork, a four-page form detailing all personal information as mandated by law. As first-time visitors, we were issued membership cards, marking our official entry into an unfamiliar but fascinating experience.

Abhishek and I chose an *AR-15 rifle with sixty rounds of ammunition*, along with a brief training session and a target sheet. I was genuinely thrilled. It had been decades since I last held a rifle, dating back to my NCC days in school and college, when we trained under the steady guidance of army instructors. That long-dormant memory stirred the moment the rifle rested in my hands again.

The safety briefing was detailed and uncompromising. Protective glasses, earmuffs, clearly marked lanes, and constant supervision ensured that every step was controlled and secure. The professionalism of the setup left a strong impression. Firearms here were treated with seriousness and respect: as instruments of sport and discipline, not chaos.

Our trainer patiently guided us through the process: how to hold the rifle, load the magazine, lock it into place, set the selector, brace the stock firmly against the shoulder, align the sights with the bull's-eye, and finally, fire a single shot. We set our target at the designated distance and began, taking turns to load and fire six rounds at a time until all sixty were spent.

The sharp crack of the first shot echoing through the range was both powerful and exhilarating. With each round, my confidence grew, my aim steadied, and the rhythm returned. It was an intense, absorbing experience: one that demanded complete presence of mind.

When we stepped out, smiling and slightly dazed, we carried our target sheet with us, the rifle returned and the faint scent of gunpowder lingering in the air. I later brought that target sheet safely back to India as a cherished souvenir. Inside, the atmosphere had been friendly and respectful, filled with enthusiasts of all ages and skill levels, united by a shared code of discipline and learning.

It turned out to be a memorable New Jersey experience: not merely about shooting, but about concentration, confidence, and stepping briefly into a different cultural space. By the end of the day, our ears rang faintly, and our thoughts grew reflective. Travel, I realised once again, is not only about witnessing beauty; it is also about understanding difference.

SoJo Spa: A Day of Rest

After so much motion, we needed a pause. The answer came in the form of *SoJo Spa Club*, perched by the Hudson in Edgewater, New Jersey. The spa was a vertical retreat: seven floors of pools, saunas, and breathtaking views of the Manhattan skyline.

A truly relaxing escape, it was nothing short of rejuvenating. The moment we stepped inside, we were greeted by a calming blend of warmth and quiet elegance. From the soothing aroma of the saunas to the soft hum of tranquillity in the infinity pool, every moment felt like a retreat from the rush of everyday life.

We spent an entire day drifting between hot stone rooms, open-air baths, and quiet lounges. The rooftop infinity pool was my favourite; floating in warm water while gazing at the New York skyline felt surreal, as if time had slowed down just for us. The city glowing across the river, its skyscrapers reflected in the calm blue water.

Neha treated us to a delicious lunch of rice, ramen noodles, and burgers at the spa's restaurant: a comforting meal that matched the restful pace of the day. Afterward, we explored the spa's many wellness experiences: a warm jacuzzi, hydrotherapy jets that massaged our backs and feet, and a variety of unique saunas and baths.

I especially loved the Himalayan salt sauna, the carbon-rich bath, the Japanese silk bath, and the Hinoki cedar bath. Each offered a different kind of comfort and calm. Among the saunas, the Ganbanyoku hot stone therapy, Far Infrared Room, and even the icy-cold Ice Room stood out; each experience left my skin glowing and my mind refreshed.

The staff were courteous and attentive, ensuring every guest felt at ease. As the sun began to set, I took one last dip in the hydrotherapy pool and watched the golden light glimmer over Manhattan.

SoJo Spa is more than just a spa; it is a sanctuary of calm where one reconnects with body, mind, and the beauty around. We left deeply relaxed and grateful for this haven so close to the city, a place where stillness felt like a luxury.

That day was less about sightseeing and more about slowing down, letting the journey catch up with us. It was another quiet moment of *experiencing America beyond postcards*. Every traveller needs a pause button: SoJo was ours.

Visit to Monster Mini Golf, Fairfield, New Jersey

Neha and Abhishek had planned a fun outing for us: a visit to *Monster Mini Golf* in Fairfield for a round of mini golf. When we arrived, we parked near a small lake surrounded by geese. To our delight, we also spotted a graceful grey stork and a pearl-white crane. Bright orange koi fish, nearly the length of an arm, glided effortlessly through the water.

Inside, a mesmerizing, *glow-in-the-dark golf course* awaited us. The entire place was lit in neon colours, with monsters and ghouls popping up unexpectedly along the 18-hole course. At one hole, a monster even swallowed a ball that Sunitha hit and, after much laughter, finally spat it out.

We bought four tickets and received glowing golf balls, clubs, a scorecard, and a pencil. Taking turns at each hole, we quickly realized that while some were easy, others were surprisingly challenging: and occasionally frustrating.

One hole required spinning a wheel and following whatever instruction appeared:

- I landed a "hole in one" but still ended up taking two shots.
- Abhishek got an extra obstacle in his path: Neha had to stand in as the obstruction.
- Neha had to play using the opposite end of the golf club.
- Sunitha had to attempt her shot from behind her back.

We laughed nonstop and took plenty of photographs along the way.

At one point, the staff suddenly played a popular song and announced that anyone who danced would receive a glowing necklace. Neha and I happily joined in and proudly earned one each.

We finally reached the 18th hole, where the challenge was to shoot the ball straight into the monster's mouth. If successful, it counted as a "hole in one;" if not, it was marked as three putts. Either way, the monster swallowed the ball, marking the end of the game. We tallied our scores, and Abhishek emerged as the winner.

Since it was also a gaming arena, Neha and Abhishek had booked a few additional games. As a bonus, we tried a 3D King Kong ride. Abhishek helped Sunitha and me with the VR headsets and instructed us to hold the safety bar firmly.

Once the ride began, it felt like stepping into a thrilling 3D movie: dinosaurs of all sizes, King Kong, forests, caves, sudden drops, roller-coaster effects, and point collections all around us. We scored 7,800 points.

Next came Skee-Ball, a points game reminiscent of the pinball-style games from our childhood. Each of us rolled balls up the inclined lane, aiming for 5,000 or 10,000 points, though we managed 2,000 instead. Still, we collected enough tickets to redeem small prizes. We also played basketball and earned more tickets, finishing with a total of 100 points.

At the counter, we exchanged them for gifts: a bouncing ball for Abhishek, a ring for Neha, a pair of hair bands for Sunitha, and a souvenir coin for me.

When it was time to leave, we walked back to the little lake where our EV was charging and took a few more photos of the birds and the peaceful surroundings. It was a simple outing, but one filled with joy, surprises, and memories that will stay with us.

Reflections and Reminiscences

"In the end, we remember not the miles we travelled, but the moments that changed us along the way."

The first chapter of any journey is about adjustment: learning how new air feels in your lungs, how grocery aisles are organised, and how time zones sneak up on your appetite. Gradually, the unfamiliar softened. The car dashboard clock was set to Eastern Time, favourite radio stations were bookmarked, and home, for now, found a new definition.

Looking back, those first few weeks set the tone for everything that followed. They taught patience, the kind that airports demand and road trips reward. They offered the quiet realization that long travel is not an escape; it is a series of small negotiations between expectation and discovery.

When I think of that arrival now, it is not the flights or the customs lines I remember, but the smaller frames: the sound of temple bells in Bridgewater, the first pink blossoms over a New Jersey sidewalk, the taste of cider after a climb, and the comforting certainty that the road ahead was long, open, and waiting.

Every journey needs a launchpad. For us, New Jersey was not merely a stop; it was the soil from which the rest of our American story grew. Each experience, distinct in its own way, stitched together the opening chapter of our journey: a chapter filled with gratitude, discovery, and quiet wonder.

As the days passed, our comfort with this new rhythm deepened, and soon excitement began to rise once more. In just a few days, we would be setting off on a weekend drive to Pennsylvania that Neha and Abhishek had planned, where waterfalls, short treks, and scenic viewpoints awaited us.

We knew the journey would bring fresh air, flowing streams, and the gentle beauty of nature, and the thought filled us with eager anticipation. With plans taking shape and spirits high, we looked forward to stepping into the next adventure, ready for the moments and memories it would add to our unfolding story.

PENNSYLVANIA:

CHASING WATERFALL'S AND MOUNTAIN TRAILS

CHAPTER 3

THE CALL OF THE CASCADES - A PENNSYLVANIA ESCAPE

"Between mountain shadows and rushing streams, Pennsylvania whispers stories only a wandering heart can hear."

Drive to a Neighbouring State

There are journeys that feel less like travel and more like quiet conversations with nature. As the season shifted and the month prepared to turn its page, we felt a gentle urge to step beyond the familiar rhythm of Jersey City and follow the call of winding roads, whispering trees, and distant falls.

As the month drew to a close, we set out on a weekend road trip to *Pennsylvania*, a journey of nearly 150 miles from Neha's home in Jersey City. The drive was scenic and refreshing, carrying us through winding highways, dense green forests, and charming small towns, making the journey as beautiful as the destinations ahead.

Crossing the majestic *Delaware River*, which forms the natural border between New Jersey and Pennsylvania, marked our entry into a state known for its rolling mountains, lush forests, and countless waterfalls. Sunlight broke through the trees in silver shards as we drove deeper into the Pocono Mountains.

Chasing Waterfalls and Mountain Trails

It was the kind of day when the sky felt wider, the air lighter, and the heart ready for discovery: a perfect moment to chase waterfalls and mountain trails across the border into Pennsylvania.

Our first stop was *Bushkill Falls*, often called *"The Niagara of Pennsylvania."* The hike along wooden bridges and forest trails was enchanting. Roaring waterfalls, framed by lush greenery, created a breathtaking sight.

Nearby, a small museum offered glimpses of early Native American life: traditional teepees, displays of local wildlife, wooden huts, and ancient hunting tools, adding a sense of history to the natural wonder.

After the trek, we treated ourselves to handmade fudge from a quaint local shop: rich chocolate and creamy cookie dough flavours that melted in the mouth.

Our next destination was *Raymondskill Falls*, another stunning cascade surrounded by tranquil greenery. The short uphill walk to its viewpoint was refreshing, and the cool, misty breeze near the falls felt invigorating. We captured several photographs from both the upper and lower viewpoints.

Lunch was simple yet deeply satisfying: homemade sandwiches lovingly packed by Neha and Abhishek. Whole-grain bread layered with veggie patties and avocado, enjoyed amidst the calm of nature, tasted all the better for the setting.

Our final stop was *Dingmans Falls*, peaceful and green, where the gentle sound of water flowing over rocks brought perfect calm to the day.

Each waterfall had its own character: Bushkill's grandeur, Raymondskill's serenity, and Dingmans' quiet simplicity. The rush of water, the crisp mountain air, and the glimmer of sunlight on the cascades made it a truly magical day in nature.

As evening descended, we began our drive back toward Jersey City, the golden light slowly fading over the Pennsylvania hills. With the hour growing late, Neha suggested a special dinner, and we stopped en route at the *Sushi Hibachi Lounge*, a Japanese live-cooking restaurant, to end the day with a warm and memorable meal.

Hibachi Meal at Sushi Hibachi Lounge

The restaurant offered more than just food; it was a performance: a lively blend of sizzling grills, joy, and artistry. Each hibachi table seats eight guests with a shared chef. We were four, and another family joined us.

We began with the classic Japanese clear soup and a crisp salad topped with a spicy dressing before our chef arrived, carrying all the ingredients for eight individual orders: no sharing allowed. We ordered three combinations of chicken, prawns, and vegetables, while Abhishek chose an all-vegetable option.

What followed was pure theatre. Our chef dazzled us with aerobics-like flair: juggling knives, tossing vegetables into the air, and building flaming onion towers that drew applause and smiles from everyone at the table. He served each of us two dipping sauces, then poured oil onto the grill, creating a brief, dramatic bonfire.

With swift, confident movements, he cracked eight eggs, added a generous pat of butter, and prepared scrambled eggs on one side of the grill while vegetables sizzled on the other. On the remaining space, he cooked a large heap of rice and noodles, mixing in butter, eggs, Japanese spices, and even a splash of sake.

He served us straight from the grill, beginning with egg fried rice. The irresistible aroma of grilled vegetables, eggs, and rice filled the air as he worked with rhythmic precision. The noodles followed in the same energetic style. Next came the chicken pieces and tiger prawns: sizzling, flipping, and perfectly seasoned.

At one point, the chef tossed cucumber chunks into the air for us to catch with our mouths. All of us failed spectacularly, and mine hilariously landed in my pocket.

He then served the noodles, followed by the vegetables. Abhishek received a generous portion of vegetables, while the rest of us were given smaller servings, as we also had prawns and chicken.

We enjoyed a delicious combination of fried rice, noodles, chicken, prawns, and vegetables tossed in flavourful sauces: every bite bursting with taste and texture. The portions were overwhelmingly generous, so we happily took home the leftovers.

After dinner, we drove to Lincoln Park and ended the night with a long, contented walk home. It was an evening of warmth, light-hearted moments, and delightful flavours: the perfect finale to a day filled with waterfalls, nature, and the simple joy of shared experiences.

Reflections and Reminiscences

There are journeys that nourish more than the senses; they restore something deep within. Our Pennsylvania escape was one such experience. The rhythm of falling water, the scent of damp earth, and the whisper of mountain winds created a quiet dialogue with nature that felt both grounding and uplifting.

Each trail invited us not just to walk through the forest, but to slow down, breathe, and reconnect with the world around us. As we moved from one waterfall to another, it became clear that travel is not merely about reaching new places; it is about rediscovering ourselves in spaces where nature speaks in its own timeless language.

Looking back, what lingers most are not just the sights, but the moments: the easy laughter during our hikes, the simple pleasure of homemade sandwiches under an open sky, the shared excitement of discovering new waterfalls, and the joyful surprise of a lively hibachi show that brought the day to a cheerful close.

These experiences stitched together a tapestry of memories richer than any itinerary. Each cascade we visited held a different mood, yet together they painted a portrait of serenity, adventure, and gratitude.

As the day ended, I realised that this simple road trip had become far more than a weekend escape. It reminded us how nature restores the spirit: through the thunder of waterfalls, the quiet strength of mountains, and the warmth of moments shared with loved ones.

Driving back under the fading light, walking through Lincoln Park, and returning home with tired feet but full hearts, I felt once again that the true joy of travel lies not only in the places we see, but in the moments we gather and the memories we carry forward.

NEW YORK CITY:

THE CITY THAT NEVER SLEEPS

CHAPTER 4

NEW YORK - THE CITY THAT NEVER SLEEPS

"In New York, the heartbeat of the world echoes in every street, every skyline, every step you take."

New York City is vibrant, magnetic, and endlessly alive. It has long captivated the imagination of travellers, and for us, it was no different. The city welcomed us with towering skyscrapers, bustling streets, and an unmistakable pulse that seemed to flow through every corner. The sounds, the lights, the people: everything moved to a rhythm entirely its own.

Our journey into this iconic metropolis began with a sense of awe that only deepened with each visit. Whether it was the dazzling spectacle of Times Square, the quiet elegance of Central Park, or the timeless silhouette of the Statue of Liberty, New York revealed itself layer by layer, moment by moment.

From the instant we stepped into the city, it felt as though we were standing at the crossroads of the world: surrounded by history, ambition, and dreams woven into steel and glass. Each day unfolded like a scene from a film, filled with memorable sights and the unmistakable charm that makes New York one of the greatest cities on earth.

If New Jersey was our calm, New York City was our pulse. Every crossing over the Hudson felt like stepping into an electric field. The moment the skyline appeared: sharp, dramatic, brimming with possibility, we could feel the city's invisible current. *You do not simply enter New York City; it engulfs you.*

New York's five boroughs: Manhattan, Brooklyn, Queens, the Bronx, and Staten Island: together form a world within a city, each with its own identity and heartbeat. *Manhattan* is the vibrant core, home to skyscrapers, theatres, and cultural landmarks. *Brooklyn* radiates creativity with its art scene, waterfront charm, and the iconic Brooklyn Bridge.

Queens, the most diverse borough, offers flavours from around the world through its neighbourhoods and cuisines. The *Bronx* proudly carries its rich history: Yankee Stadium and the birthplace of hip-hop among its defining symbols. *Staten Island*, calm and scenic, provides a quieter retreat with parks, beaches, and sweeping views of the skyline.

Together, these boroughs weave New York's ever-evolving story: a city that celebrates diversity, energy, and endless possibility.

Sunitha and I visited New York City several times with our daughter Neha and our son-in-law Abhishek. Each trip to a new borough endeared the city to us a little more.

Some visits were bright, busy days; others were late nights spent by the waterfront, watching ferries drift quietly across the dark river. Each light, each ripple, felt like another heartbeat in the vast rhythm of the city.

Moments in Motion

New York City was never about a single attraction; it was a collage of small, unforgettable moments:

- The rush of air as the subway roared past underground murals.
- The warm perfume of roasted chestnuts drifting through Bryant Park.
- The brief, kind nod of a stranger sharing shelter during an unexpected drizzle.
- A child in Central Park chasing bubbles that floated toward the skyscrapers.

The city taught us to look closer, to find stories in every corner. We began naming our days not by what we saw, but by what we felt: *the laughter day, the drizzle day, the pizza day.*

Every visit began with a small ritual. We would walk from our home in Jersey City to the Journal Square PATH Station, clutch our travel cards, and wait for the train that always seemed five minutes late: yet somehow, always right on time. The ride itself was a quiet transformation, shifting from Jersey City's industrial-residential mix into the long, dark tunnel that carried us beneath Manhattan's restless heart.

First Steps into the City

No matter how long you stay near New York City, there is an invisible magnet pulling you toward it. Our first major city day arrived with equal parts excitement and expectation. We boarded the train at Journal Square PATH Station in New Jersey, navigated the tangle of stations, and emerged onto 33rd Street: the heartbeat of Manhattan.

The first time we stepped out, sunlight ricocheted off glass towers like music. The air carried the scent of roasted nuts mixed with subway heat. Street vendors juggled pretzels and hot dogs, while taxi horns layered themselves into the city's constant background score.

Manhattan Mornings and Macy's Afternoons

We stood still for a moment, simply watching. Everything moved fast, yet nobody seemed to hurry. New York possessed a paradoxical intimacy: a city of millions that somehow felt personal. It is impossible to be neutral about New York City: it demands a reaction. The streets pulsed with movement: yellow cabs darting like impatient wasps, vendors calling out, skyscrapers rising like unanswered questions.

Our first stop was *Macy's Herald Square*, more legend than store: a temple of shopping and history. Floor after floor of fashion, perfume, and festive displays greeted us with almost theatrical energy.

We were fortunate to visit during the Spring Flower Show. After the chill of winter, New York awakens each year with a spectacular celebration of colour, as Macy's Herald Square transforms into an enchanting indoor garden. This grand floral exhibition turns one of the world's busiest department stores into a living canvas of spring.

As we stepped through the revolving doors, the familiar scent of perfume and polished marble gave way to something magical: a wave of fragrance, colour, and creativity. Everywhere we looked, blossoms spilled from elaborate displays: tulips, orchids, roses, hydrangeas, and lilies arranged in dramatic cascades and sculptures. Peacocks, butterflies, and fountains rose from seas of flowers, and the air felt perfumed with spring itself. For me, it was more than a flower show; it was an experience of optimism and wonder, a living tapestry woven into the heart of Manhattan.

Inside, escalators creaked like old bones, and perfume counters glittered beneath soft lights. We rode the historic wooden escalator, marvelling at how something could feel both antique and modern. Each floor felt like its own kingdom: fashion, kitchenware, and quiet corners where staff chatted casually about Broadway shows.

By midday, we made our way to Bryant Park and found a bench where we shared Korean rice cakes and waffles with cream that Neha had brought for us. A man strummed a guitar nearby, children chased one another across the lawn, and tourists wandered lazily through the pathways. Slowly, the rhythm of the city settled into our bones.

By lunchtime, we had fully surrendered to New York's pulse. We watched the world whirl around us: office workers striding with purpose, chess players leaning intently over their boards, pigeons fluttering in hopeful circles. Every scene flowed seamlessly into the city's vibrant energy, and we found ourselves quiet observers within a living, breathing symphony.

Exploring New York City's West Side Wonders:

World Trade Centre Station, Chelsea Market, and the Walk to the Vessel

On our next visit, we travelled from *Journal Square PATH Station* in New Jersey and arrived at the famous *World Trade Center (WTC) Station* in New York City. The experience was both emotional and awe-inspiring. Known as the *Oculus*, this architectural masterpiece designed by Santiago Calatrava stands as a powerful symbol of resilience and renewal after the events of 9/11. Its soaring white wings and vast open interior are flooded with natural light, creating a sense of hope and calm amid the city's constant motion.

As I walked through its gleaming corridors lined with shops and cafes, I was struck by how seamlessly the space connects to the *9/11 Memorial and Museum*, gently blending remembrance with everyday life. The grand design, marked by graceful symmetry and a serene atmosphere, reminded me that New York does not merely rebuild: it reimagines, standing tall as a tribute to human strength and spirit.

From there, we headed to New York City's Chelsea district, an unforgettable journey through creativity, culture, and urban beauty. Our exploration began at *Chelsea Market*, where we wandered through its lively indoor spaces. The historic brick building buzzed with energy, a perfect fusion of old industrial charm and modern design.

Chelsea Market is a true food lover's paradise, offering cuisines from around the world under one iconic roof. As we strolled through its bustling corridors, aromas of freshly baked bread, sizzling seafood, and gourmet coffee filled the air. From lobster rolls, sushi, and tacos to pasta, pastries, and falafel, every stall told a story of craftsmanship and flavour. Desserts followed naturally: artisanal chocolates, creamy gelato, and rich cheesecakes tempting every passerby.

Neha took us to a stall called *Very Fresh Noodles*, where she ordered a takeaway box of delicious noodles for us. We then visited the famous *Los Tacos No. 1*, sampling several varieties, including a cactus (nopal) taco: a first for us. Enjoyed piping hot at a nearby table, they were truly delicious. To complete the culinary trail, we treated ourselves to masala chai at *Chotey Miya*, an Indian tea stall that felt wonderfully familiar.

From Chelsea Market, we walked toward Pier 57, where the rooftop park offered sweeping views of the Manhattan skyline. Nearby, *Little Island* rose like a floating garden, a striking architectural marvel with lush landscaping and gently curved walkways.

Our journey continued along the *High Line*: a stunning elevated park built on a former railway track. The pathway wove between art installations, green spaces, and glass towers, offering a fresh and ever-changing perspective of the city's west side.

Our final stop was the *Vessel* at Hudson Yards, a dramatic honeycomb-like structure symbolizing modern design and imagination. Climbing its interlocking stairways is currently permitted for a fee, though entry is free on Thursdays for New York City residents and children under five with valid ID. Those who make the climb are rewarded with panoramic views of the skyline and the Hudson River below.

The entire Chelsea and Hudson Yards experience was a perfect blend of art, innovation, and nature: a testament to how New York City continually reinvents itself.

New York Food Tour - Flavors and Footsteps through Downtown

Next on our list was a *Walking Food Tour* planned by Abhishek and Neha, who became our guides this time, having experienced a similar guided tour earlier.

Our first stop was *L'Industrie Pizzeria* in the Village. The queue outside must be seen to be believed: stretching seemingly endlessly down the street. After nearly an hour, we finally made it inside and ordered three generous slices: Margherita, Burrata Cheese, and Tartufo Mushroom. While waiting, we enjoyed gelato drizzled with olive oil and sprinkled with salt, watching the chefs work with impressive speed and precision.

The pizzas were truly worth the wait: one of the tastiest highlights of our New York food trail. The aroma of freshly baked dough, the crisp yet soft crust, and the perfect balance of cheese and tomato sauce made every bite unforgettable. This modest little spot carries a big reputation, and it was easy to understand why locals and visitors alike patiently queue for a slice.

From there, we walked to the iconic *Friends* TV *show apartment building* in Greenwich Village. Standing there felt surreal, like stepping into television history: a delightful pop-culture moment that paired perfectly with great food, both experiences uniquely New York.

Our culinary adventure continued with an delightful mix of flavours and discoveries. Next was *Ficco's Italian Restaurant*, where we savoured rice, potato, and cheese balls, cheese ravioli with rich sauces, and comforting homestyle pasta. Their warm hospitality reminded us of family dinners back home.

A short walk away was *Murray's Cheese*, a paradise for cheese lovers. We sampled aged cheddar, creamy brie, and mozzarella so fresh it nearly melted in my hand. We finished with their signature mac and cheese: rich, indulgent, and deeply satisfying.

Then came *Molly's Cupcakes*, which brought out the child in all of us with its cheerful decor and generous swirls of frosting. We ordered two flavours: chocolate with peanut butter and pista rose, both delightful and memorable.

At *Pomme Frites*, our next stop, we could not resist the golden Belgian-style fries served with an array of dips. We selected three, and the result was simple yet irresistible comfort food.

Pizza appeared once again on our list, this time at *Bleecker Street Pizza*, another celebrated joint. We tried three slices: chipotle chicken and cheese, Sicilian tomato, and plain cheese, along with a plate of garlic knots served with spicy marinara sauce. Everything was delicious.

A visit to *Raffetto's* added yet another dimension to the day. Watching fresh pasta being hand-cut and sold by weight felt like stepping into a century-old Italian kitchen. By this point, we were thoroughly full, so we skipped tasting and opted for takeaway instead. A quick stop at a nearby grocery store for lemonade helped us recover.

To burn off some calories, we ended the day with a leisurely stroll through *Washington Square Park*. Adjacent to New York University, the park was alive with energy: it was convocation day, and students in formal attire mingled with proud parents and well-wishers.

Near the park entrance, several elderly gentlemen sat at small chess and Scrabble tables, inviting passersby to play. The sight brought back memories of my brothers, both excellent chess players. Dancers, musicians, lively cafés, and street art filled the park, capturing the youthful heartbeat of the city.

It was a journey that satisfied every sense, from the aroma of cheese and pasta to the artistic streets of downtown Manhattan: truly a celebration of culture, taste, and timeless New York charm.

Roosevelt Island and Tramway Ride

Roosevelt Island, a narrow strip in the East River between *Manhattan and Queens*, offered one of the most unique and memorable experiences of our New York visit. *Riding the Roosevelt Island Tramway* was like gliding through a living postcard.

Suspended high above the river, the tram moved gracefully between Manhattan and the island, offering spectacular views of the downtown skyline, the Queensboro Bridge, and the glittering waters below. Though the ride lasted only about three minutes, it felt like soaring over the city itself.

Once on the island, we explored the pier and admired the Queens downtown skyline. Historic landmarks, including the haunting remains of the Smallpox Hospital and nearby research institutes, spoke to Roosevelt Island's rich past, blending history, education, and scenic calm in a surprisingly compact space.

We boarded the *Red Free Bus*, which loops around the island: a convenient and fun way to explore. At the northern tip, we stepped off to visit *Lighthouse Park*, where an old stone lighthouse stands proudly overlooking the river. Nearby, the *"Girl's Face" sculptures* added an artistic touch to the serene setting, creating the perfect photo opportunity.

On the return journey, the bus took us back to the southern end near *Cornell Tech University*. The modern architecture and riverside location gave the campus a peaceful, academic atmosphere. We stopped at the cafeteria for a quiet snack of yogurt, potato chips, and a sweet bun with filling. Later, we sat watching the tram glide across the skyline once more: a fitting end to a calm, captivating, and quietly magical island adventure right in the heart of New York City.

A Serene Day on Staten Island: Journey by the Ferry

Our day visit to Staten Island began with a scenic ride on the *Staten Island Ferry*, one of New York's most iconic experiences. Operating all day, every day (less frequency on holidays and weekends), and free of charge, the ferry offers a unique way to take in the city's skyline.

As we glided across the Hudson, the *Statue of Liberty* stood gracefully against the horizon, while Lower Manhattan receded behind us: a view both calming and unforgettable. The cool river breeze, the gentle hum of the ferry, and the golden sunlight dancing on the water made the journey feel quietly magical.

Upon arrival, we explored the St. George neighbourhood, where the Staten Island Museum and cozy local cafes lent a relaxed, small-town charm just minutes from Manhattan's relentless energy. A stroll along the waterfront revealed the serene rhythm of island life: open spaces, greenery, and the rare luxury of slowing down.

Our walk through the Snug Harbor Cultural Center and Botanical Garden unveiled beautifully curated gardens, historic architecture, and art exhibits, reflecting the borough's creative spirit. As evening approached, we returned on the ferry, watching the sun set behind the Statue of Liberty while Manhattan's skyline began to twinkle—a perfect finale to a refreshing and memorable day on Staten Island.

Walking the Iconic Brooklyn Bridge: A Journey Between Two Boroughs

We returned from Staten Island by ferry, walked to the WTC station, and took a connecting subway train to *Brooklyn*. The borough greeted us with its creative pulse and neighbourhood warmth. Crossing the iconic *Brooklyn Bridge* on foot was a highlight, the skyline unfolding behind us as the wind brushed across the East River. Walking across this magnificent structure, I felt the perfect blend of history, engineering marvel, and breathtaking beauty.

The bridge's grand stone towers and intricate cables stood proudly against the sky, connecting two vibrant boroughs: Manhattan and Brooklyn, while silently telling stories of the past. As I moved along the wooden pathway, I captured several photos of the Manhattan skyline ahead and the shimmering East River below, reflecting the city's endless energy.

The walk was about more than just the view; it was the feeling of being part of something timeless and inspiring. Locals jogged past, tourists paused for photos, and street musicians filled the air with melody, adding life to the bridge's atmosphere.

Beneath the bridge, we enjoyed a delicious Thai meal at *Elephant District*, followed by ice cream from the famous *Brooklyn Ice Cream Factory*. Later, we photographed the bridge by night and wandered to the pebble beach below, soaking in the lovely view.

Our exploration continued in DUMBO (*Down Under the Manhattan Bridge Overpass*), with its cobblestone streets, charming cafes, and riverside park. Standing there, looking back at the bridge glowing in the evening light, I understood why it remains one of New York's most beloved landmarks: a symbol of connection, resilience, and the city's enduring spirit.

From the historic charm of Brooklyn Heights to the vibrant energy of Williamsburg, the borough effortlessly blended tradition with modern artistry. Every corner seemed alive with culture, music, and imagination, a perfect complement to Manhattan's bustling energy.

Icons of Midtown Manhattan: Library, Cathedral, and Grand Central

After an early weekday lunch, we set out to explore some of Manhattan's most iconic landmarks. Our journey through midtown felt like a walk through living history, where elegant architecture and vibrant culture define the heart of New York City.

The *New York Public Library* stood gracefully on Fifth Avenue, its marble lions: *Patience* and *Fortitude*, guarding the grand entrance. Stepping inside felt like entering a sanctuary of knowledge and grace. The vast reading room glowed beneath ornate chandeliers, lined with shelves of treasured books and studious readers. The calm of the library felt almost sacred, a gentle escape from the city's constant motion.

The library's three floors of marble staircases, high arched windows, and hushed corridors exuded old-world charm. The highlight was the magnificent Rose Main Reading Room, stretching the length of a city block. Carved oak tables, towering bookshelves, and golden chandeliers glowed softly against the painted ceiling clouds. Scholars, tourists, and locals sat quietly immersed in their work, their focus blending with the serene atmosphere. It was more than a library; it felt like the soul of New York, where history, architecture, and intellect met in perfect harmony.

From there, we walked a few blocks to the *St. Patrick's Cathedral*, its Gothic spires reaching heavenward amidst modern skyscrapers. The detailed stone carvings, stunning stained-glass windows, and peaceful interiors left a lasting impression. Inside, the rush of the outside world faded, replaced by quiet reverence. We gave a donation, lit candles, sat in the pews, and were fortunate to witness a mass in progress: a truly heavenly experience.

Our next stop was the magnificent *Grand Central Station*, a living monument to New York's spirit. Beneath its celestial ceiling mural, crowds moved with rhythmic grace. This station is far more than a railway terminal; it is a breathing piece of the city's history and heart. I was awestruck by the marble concourse crowned by the famous turquoise ceiling, painted with constellations twinkling faintly in the soft light.

The grand clock atop the information booth gleamed beneath the chandeliers, a silent witness to countless arrivals and farewells. Majestic arched windows and marble halls captured both sophistication and the unstoppable energy of a city forever on the move. I couldn't help but exclaim, *"Wow, it is so beautiful!"* It felt less like a train station and more like a grand architectural marvel; almost a mall in its scale and elegance. We took pictures and wandered around, marvelling at the sheer number of people flowing in every direction. No wonder it is considered the world's largest train station, both in area and in the number of platforms.

Commuters and travellers moved with purpose, yet there was an unspoken rhythm that made the hustle feel graceful. The whispering gallery, hidden corners of gourmet markets, and art deco details all added to its charm. Standing there, I felt connected to generations of people who had passed through, each carrying their own stories, hopes, and destinations.

Neha reminded us of the famous *Magnolia Bakery* just below, renowned for its banana pudding. We indulged in its rich, creamy sweetness, a delightful treat that perfectly concluded our Midtown explorations.

The Green Calm and the Dazzling Glow: Central Park and Times Square

On our next visit, leaving architectural wonders behind, we spent time in *Central Park*, New York City's sprawling green haven. The fresh air and natural beauty offered a welcome pause from the city's relentless pace. Established in 1858, Central Park spans 843 acres and was the first landscaped public park in the United States.

The park was alive with movement and colour. Beautiful statues, bridges, fountains, and street singers dotted the landscape. Visitors cycled, walked, jogged, and enjoyed leisurely horse-drawn carriage rides or three-wheel cycles. Towering trees provided shade, while slender skyscrapers: some as thin as pencils, rose dramatically beyond the park's borders. We were told this stretch is known as *Billionaires' Row,* a striking contrast between wealth and wilderness.

At *Bow Bridge and Bethesda Terrace,* I lingered to watch reflections ripple across the water and to listen to the soft music of street performers. We witnessed several couples proposing, each moment carefully captured by personal photographers celebrating their joy.

The park felt like the city's breathing space: alive yet calm, where nature and human life blended effortlessly. We spotted ducks and geese gliding across the water, squirrels darting between trees, a family of raccoons climbing high branches, and even clusters of turtles basking in the sun. A lady sitting patiently feeding the turtles bits of hotdog.

As dusk melted into night, the city's rhythm carried us to *Times Square.* The transformation was immediate and overwhelming. We were enveloped by a dazzling sea of lights, sound, and colour. Towering digital billboards lit up the sky, flashing advertisements and Broadway show signs, turning the square into a modern-day carnival.

Street performers, costumed characters, and excited tourists filled every corner. Music spilled from nearby stores, laughter echoed through the crowds, and the city's pulse throbbed with unstoppable energy. Standing there, surrounded by it all, I felt both small and exhilarated: as if witnessing New York's heartbeat at its brightest. Times Square truly embodied the city's spirit: vibrant, chaotic, and endlessly alive.

Reflections and Reminiscences

New York's greatest gift, we realised after several weekends of crossing in and out of its streets, is not its monuments or museums, but its ability to make you feel awake: truly awake, in a way few places can.

It does not ask you to love it; instead, it challenges you to keep up, to stay curious, to surrender to its rhythm. And somewhere in the quiet act of trying to match its pace, you find yourself falling in love with it, piece by piece.

As we moved from borough to borough: sharing simple meals, marvelling at architecture, tasting global cuisines, and walking miles through history and modernity, I realised the city is not defined by its skyline alone; it is defined by its pulse. Every street corner held a story, every neighbourhood carried a personality, and every subway ride stitched us closer to the fabric of the city.

What made it even more special was watching Neha and Abhishek guide us through places that were once new to them too. Their excitement, familiarity, and thoughtful planning made the city feel not just grand, but personal. In their company, even crowded streets felt warm, and hectic days felt easy. It reminded me that travel is as much about the people you journey with as the places you see.

New York is honest. No one pretends here. Artists share sidewalks with bankers; students brush past executives; dreamers walk alongside cynics. In the swirl of faces, accents, and ambitions, the city teaches you to see people not as strangers, but as stories.

You begin to walk faster, think sharper, and embrace the unexpected. And even when you leave, the city's heartbeat stays with you: a steady reminder to keep moving, keep seeking, and keep hoping.

What stayed with us most were not the famous sights, but the moments between them: children chasing one another beneath skyscrapers, a guitarist playing under a bridge, the kindness of a stranger holding a door a heartbeat longer. In those fleeting encounters, the city revealed its soul. Standing beneath the soaring wings of the Oculus, watching sunsets from Staten Island, or sitting quietly in Central Park as raccoons scampered by, I felt connected to something larger: a reminder of how creativity and resilience shape extraordinary spaces.

From the dazzling chaos of Times Square to a peaceful coffee at a streetside café, Manhattan captured the spirit of endless movement and possibility.

As our train rolled back toward New Jersey one night, the skyline softened behind us, glowing like a distant promise. I pressed my forehead to the window and whispered, *I'll be back.* Because New York had done what it does best: it had taken a small piece of us and replaced it with its own, a little courage, a little wonder, and a renewed appetite for exploration.

It struck me then that travel is not about crossing continents, but about noticing how sunlight falls differently on faces that carry other stories. New York made us more attentive, more grateful, more alive.

And perhaps most importantly, it strengthened us for the journeys ahead: the long circuits that would soon take us to Chicago, Washington D.C., the West Coast, and beyond.

New York was not just a chapter in our journey. It was a teacher, a spark, and a reminder that the world is far bigger: and far more beautiful than we often allow ourselves to imagine.

CHICAGO:

FAMILY, LANDMARKS, AND MEMORIES

CHAPTER 5

MIDWEST INTERLUDE: CHICAGO AND NAPERVILLE

"Every journey carries a hush between its chapters, a moment where the world slows just enough for us to hear ourselves again."

After weeks of vibrant city lights, long drives, and countless snapshots of the East Coast, it was time to turn westward: to a place known for its winds, waters, and wide Midwestern smiles. Our next stop: *Chicago,* the city of architecture, jazz, and a skyline that seems to rise straight out of Lake Michigan's blue heart.

Sunitha's cousin, Preethi, and her family lived in Naperville and had been inviting us for several years. We were happy to finally visit their beautiful home for a few days and enjoy their warm hospitality during our stay in the USA.

Flight into the Heartland

We left home in Jersey City by bus to Journal Square Station, took the PATH train to 23rd Street in New York City, then continued by local train and finally a cab to reach *LaGuardia Airport* in Queens. There, we bid goodbye to our darling daughter, who had come to see us off at the ever-bustling gateway where goodbyes echo through bright glass corridors.

The flight to Chicago was short, but the transition felt immense: New York's chaos giving way to an expansive calm. As the plane began its descent, I caught my first glimpse of Lake Michigan stretching endlessly, reflecting the afternoon sun like a sheet of silver.

At *O'Hare International Airport,* a chill breeze greeted us even in summer. Chicago's air felt different: cooler, cleaner, and somehow less hurried. Our cousin met us at the arrivals gate with familiar warmth, her laughter melting away our travel fatigue. It felt good to belong again, even if just for a few days.

On the drive home, she took us to *Panera Bread*, known for its fresh sandwiches and hearty soups. We enjoyed delicious sandwiches and smoothies before finally arriving at their lovely house in Naperville.

Naperville: A Suburban Embrace

Our home for the next few days was *Naperville*, a peaceful suburban town west of Chicago. Tree-lined streets, perfectly mowed lawns, and little American flags fluttering on porches made it a postcard of calm after the sensory storm of New York City.

Each morning began with strong coffee and sunlight spilling through wide windows. Walks around the quiet neighbourhood became small meditations, accompanied by the rhythmic chirping of birds, the scent of freshly cut grass, and children cycling past in cheerful packs. We saw several squirrels: huge ones; I initially mistook them for mongooses.

Downtown Naperville, with its boutique shops and charming Riverwalk, quickly became a favourite. The gentle hum of water along the DuPage River, the easy warmth of families, and the inviting aroma of local bakeries gave the town a comforting heartbeat. We lingered in cafés, exchanging stories, sipping lattes, and savouring time itself.

Evenings were spent with relatives, sharing meals, talking about India, and laughing over old photographs. Travel, I realized, was not only about places; it was about reconnecting the threads of belonging across oceans.

The Art Institute of Chicago: Where Time Stands Still

Sunitha and I began our first major city outing with a visit to *The Art Institute of Chicago*, one of the oldest and most beautiful museums in America. The grand lions guarding its entrance seemed to roar silently with pride as we walked in. Inside, the air carried a hushed reverence: paintings, sculptures, and light all intertwined in quiet conversation.

The museum spanned several floors filled with magnificent art and sculptures from across the world. I was pleasantly surprised to find an entire *Asian Wing* showcasing Indian idols of deities such as Shiva, Ganesha, and Nataraja, along with serene representations of the Buddha. We wandered through the galleries for nearly four hours, completely absorbed in the beauty and history around us.

Standing before Monet's *Water Lilies* felt like standing inside a dream. The colours shimmered and breathed, as if the canvas itself were alive. Van Gogh's *The Bedroom* radiated intimacy, while Grant Wood's *American Gothic* stared back with timeless irony.

But it wasn't just the masters that impressed, it was the way the museum created space for quiet reflection. Sitting on a bench before a vast canvas, surrounded by centuries of art, I felt the strange sensation of being both a traveller and a timeless witness.

We saw several art students with sketchbooks, accompanied by their teachers, seated peacefully as they sketched sculptures at various locations throughout the museum.

We ended the day with a lovely dinner at a pizza joint called *Paradise Park Pizza and Patio* along with our cousin Preethi, her husband Murali, their daughter Manisha, and son-in-law Chris.

Shedd Aquarium: Beneath the Surface

The next day's plan was a visit to the *Shedd Aquarium*, a world beneath the water and one of Chicago's most beloved attractions. Our cousin had booked tickets in advance for this remarkable aquatic world.

As we stepped inside, the hum of the city faded into an oceanic calm. Giant tanks glowed with blue light, and schools of fish moved like liquid choreography. It felt less like an aquarium and more like a rainforest beneath glass, with every species imaginable: from the tiniest fish to majestic beluga whales. Sharks, penguins, otters, stingrays, and even a live dolphin show kept us spellbound.

We saw plankton, sea urchins, sea anemones, frogs, tarantula spiders, a baby boa snake, lobsters, and even piranhas. Visitors could touch stingrays and starfish or walk through the penguin enclosure. It is probably the best aquarium-cum-rainforest in the world I have ever seen. Watching a sea turtle glide gracefully past the glass was unforgettable, its movement so serene that time itself seemed to slow.

Exploring the City: Big Bus Tour and the Skyline

To capture Chicago's spirit, we joined the *Big Bus City Tour*, an open-top ride that winds through the city's most iconic landmarks. As the bus moved along Michigan Avenue, our guide's voice danced through the speakers, blending history and humour in equal measure.

It was one of the most enjoyable ways to explore the city, offering a panoramic view of Chicago's celebrated highlights. From the shimmering blue of Lake Michigan and the historic Navy Pier to the grandeur of The Art Institute and the architectural marvels along Michigan Avenue, every turn revealed something beautiful.

The bus first took us to Millennium Park, where the famous *Cloud Gate sculpture* gleamed in the sun. Stepping off to see *The Bean*, as everyone fondly calls it, we admired its mirrored surface reflecting the sky, the city, and our smiling faces: merging all three into one seamless image. We took photographs, of course, but the real joy lay in watching others marvel, laugh, and wave at their distorted reflections.

We then rode toward the bustling Magnificent Mile, lined with chic stores and cafés. Crossing the Chicago River, we admired the stunning skyline: a harmony of glass and steel. The Willis Tower, once the tallest building in the world, rose proudly above the city, while the Tribune Tower and the art-deco Carbide and Carbon Building added old-world charm.

No trip to Chicago is complete without tasting its world-famous deep-dish pizza, and our guide ensured the bus stopped conveniently near one of the city's icons, *Giordano's*. The aroma of freshly baked dough and melted cheese was irresistible.

The slice was a masterpiece: a thick, buttery crust overflowing with layers of mozzarella, tangy tomato sauce, and rich fillings that made every bite unforgettable. It wasn't just a meal; it was a true Chicago experience: warm, hearty, and full of flavour. Refreshed and satisfied, we hopped back on the Big Bus, taking in the last few sights before being picked up by our cousin for the drive home.

Moments of Warmth and Leisure

The Midwest pace was slower and friendlier. People smiled easily, held doors open, and genuinely asked how your day was. Our days in Chicago and Naperville unfolded gently, with morning coffee, long drives along the lakeshore, and spontaneous detours to parks and ice-cream shops.

One evening, we gathered on the patio under string lights, a gentle wind rustling through the trees. Stories flowed and laughter echoed into the soft summer night. There was no rush, no itinerary: just a rare peace that travel seldom affords.

Visit to the Chicago Balaji Temple and Our Eventful Return Journey

We woke up at 7:30 a.m., enjoyed a warm cup of tea, and savoured the delicious waffles Preethi made for breakfast, served with jam and ginger pickle, followed later by a comforting Starbucks coffee. Soon after, we drove to the *Chicago Balaji Temple*, this time, in the wonderful company of our cousin's husband, Murali who was an encyclopaedia of knowledge. He can speak about virtually anything, and his vast understanding of diverse subjects made our conversations truly enjoyable. During the drive, I was fascinated to learn that he had even trained to fly a two-seater aircraft and had clocked 70 hours of flying.

The temple was serene and beautiful, and we had a peaceful darshan, followed by prasadam: ladoo and almonds, that tasted absolutely divine. We then drove back home, carrying with us a sense of calm and contentment from the visit.

Back home, Preethi served a delightful homemade lunch: peas pulao, capsicum dal, chicken gravy, mixed vegetable curry, and crisp pappad.

Later, Sunitha, Preethi, and I went for a walk around the neighbourhood, but the cold, windy weather pushed us back indoors within minutes. While the others rested, I relaxed on their massage chair: my daily indulgence during this trip, before finishing the final round of packing.

Our return flight from Chicago to New Jersey was originally scheduled for 5:38 p.m., but shifting weather at Newark Airport caused repeated delays: to 6:33 p.m., then 7:30 p.m., and finally 8:30 p.m.

We said our warm goodbyes to Preethi and Murali, grateful for their generous hospitality, city tours, airport pickups, and drop-offs. Preethi drove us to the airport at 6 p.m. in their BMW; soon after, we checked in, cleared security, and reached the gate.

The aircraft pushed back at 8:35 p.m., but just before reaching the runway, another weather delay halted us. Eventually, by God's grace, we took off at 9:30 p.m. The journey was turbulent, even high above the clouds, leaving us anxious about when we would finally reach home.

At 11:15 p.m., the pilot announced a diversion to Atlantic City due to low fuel and worsening weather, an unexpected twist. Moments later came relief: Newark granted landing clearance as conditions improved, and the aircraft turned back.

We touched down at Newark close to midnight. Despite their own exhaustion and driving through heavy rain, Neha and Abhishek came to pick us up in a Nissan Kicks. By 1 a.m., we were finally home: tired, hungry, but deeply grateful. After a warm late-night dinner and a little catching up, we drifted to sleep at 3 a.m., bringing a truly memorable journey to a close.

Reflections and Reminiscences

Looking back, our days in Chicago and Naperville felt like a gentle pause in the middle of our journey: a perfect blend of family warmth, cultural discovery, and Midwestern calm.

Whether wandering through world-class museums, watching city lights shimmer against Lake Michigan, or enjoying quiet suburban mornings filled with coffee and sunlight, every moment carried its own quiet beauty.

The hospitality of our cousins, the laughter shared across dinner tables, and the unexpected twists of travel came together to create memories far richer than any itinerary could promise. Chicago gave us more than sights; it offered a renewed sense of belonging, gratitude, and the comforting reminder that home can exist wherever love and warmth greet you at the door.

To me, Chicago was a bridge: a pause between the rush of the East Coast and the grand adventures awaiting us in the West. It was a city that balanced strength with softness, ambition with warmth. In its architecture, I saw confidence; in its people, kindness; in its great lake, infinity.

As we packed our bags for the return trip, our restful days in Chicago and Naperville gently shifted from stillness to anticipation. With our hearts full of family warmth and our minds enriched by the city's art, architecture, and lakeside charm, we turned toward the adventures that lay ahead.

Before us stretched an 18-day journey across the East and West Coasts of the United States: a sweeping exploration of iconic cities, breathtaking landscapes, and unforgettable moments. Carrying a renewed sense of gratitude and excitement, we felt ready to embrace the next chapter of our coast-to-coast travels with open hearts and eager footsteps.

COAST - TO - COAST JOURNEY:

CROSSING THE EAST AND WEST: 18 UNFORGETTABLE DAYS

CHAPTER 6

THE GREAT AMERICAN EXPEDITION: CROSSING THE EAST AND WEST IN 18 UNFORGETTABLE DAYS

"Every journey begins with a single step and ends with countless memories."

Every great journey transforms something deep within. For us, that transformation unfolded over eighteen unforgettable days on a coast-to-coast expedition across the United States. Arranged by Chariot Travels, Bangalore, the trip became a seamless blend of history, adventure, and wonder: an experience that stitched together the very soul of America and left us with memories to cherish for a lifetime.

From the towering skyscrapers of New York to the glowing canyons of Arizona, from Hollywood dreams to Florida sunshine, this journey was not just about places. It was about feeling a nation's rhythm: its pulse, pride, and poetry.

Our tour group, consisting of thirty-eight members, began its adventure from Bangalore and landed at JFK, New York. Six of us, already in the United States, joined them at the luxurious Embassy Suites by Hilton in Parsippany, New Jersey. Our tour manager, Mr. Nalin Patel from Chariot Travels, accompanied us throughout the journey, ensuring everything ran smoothly.

We had opted for an all-inclusive package covering four-star accommodations, internal flights, luxury coaches, meals, sightseeing entry tickets, ferry rides, and professional guides wherever required. The tour was impeccably organized, and we were truly delighted with every aspect of the experience.

Our itinerary spanned the length and breadth of the country: *New York City - Washington D.C. - Hershey's (Pennsylvania) – Niagara (Buffalo) – Los Angeles – Las Vegas – Arizona (Grand Canyon) – San Francisco – Orlando – Miami – New York City.*

The final days before departure were filled with excitement: packing clothes to suit every climate, double-checking passports, debit cards, and dollars, and arranging all our travel essentials. Neha and Abhishek lovingly packed snacks for us, adding a comforting touch of home to the journey ahead.

The Journey Begins

I called our tour manager to check on the group's arrival status. Since we had arrived in the United States a month earlier to stay with Neha and Abhishek, we would be joining the group only from their first day in America. He informed me that the flight from Bangalore had landed safely at JFK Airport and that all thirty-eight members had cleared immigration. They were expected to reach the hotel by bus within thirty minutes.

Before leaving Neha's home in New Jersey, we shared four delicious pies Abhishek had bought: peach, mango, chocolate, and peanut. Each one was truly delightful. Soon after, we set out and reached the Embassy Suites by Hilton in Parsippany, New Jersey: the place where our long-awaited tour would officially begin. The property appeared calm and welcoming, but as the group's bus pulled in, my heart grew a little heavy.

Neha and Abhishek hugged us goodbye and headed back home, leaving us with a tender mix of excitement for the days ahead and the familiar ache that comes each time parents' part from their children.

Our tour manager greeted everyone and assigned the rooms. The hotel's interiors were elegant, spacious, and inviting. Our room, number 326 on the third floor, felt almost like a small suite: a cozy sofa set, a dining area with a table and two chairs, two wash basins, a coffee maker, a fridge, and a microwave. The bedroom featured a comfortable double bed with lamps on either side and a large curtained window offering a pleasant view. We were given two key cards along with login details for the hotel's free Wi-Fi.

After placing our luggage in the room, Sunitha and I stepped out for a gentle walk around the hotel grounds, which included a wide parking area and an open space in front. On returning, we freshened up, unpacked, and later spoke to Neha and Abhishek before going to sleep.

Even on the very first night, we missed them. After spending an entire month together, their absence felt immediate. Sunitha and I had been deeply touched by the beautiful camaraderie and gentle chemistry Neha and Abhishek shared: their care, thoughtfulness, and effortless coordination in everything they did.

They ensured we always had something to enjoy, whether sightseeing, indoor activities, gym time, or visits to the game room on rainy days. Their love and thoughtful planning had made every moment with them truly memorable.

Days 1–2: New York – Where the Dream Begins

"If you can make it here, you can make it anywhere." — Frank Sinatra

Our odyssey began in *New York City*, the metropolis that hums with ambition even at dawn. A guided tour introduced us to its contrasts: steel and serenity, chaos and charm; all coexisting in a rhythm uniquely its own.

The day began with an excellent buffet breakfast at our hotel. I ordered the chef's special chicken-and-cheese double omelette with cranberry juice, while Sunitha enjoyed orange juice, pastries, and fresh fruit. With a small box of yogurt packed for later, we boarded the bus toward Liberty State Park. An accident on the highway prompted our driver to take an alternate route: a happy and surprising detour that took us right past Neha and Abhishek's apartment in Jersey City.

The Torch of Hope: Our Time with Lady Liberty

At Liberty State Park, we boarded the *Statue City Cruises ferry*, the only one permitted to carry visitors to *Liberty and Ellis Islands.* From the top deck, the Statue of Liberty slowly emerged through the soft haze, her torch steady against the harbour wind.

A quiet awe settled over everyone, stirred not merely by the monument itself, but by the promise she represents: freedom, hope, and the dreams of millions.

Up close, *Lady Liberty* was breathtaking. Her weathered green patina spoke of time and endurance. We admired the golden flame of her torch and the tablet inscribed with the date of American independence. At the Liberty Museum, we learned about her journey from France and the careful assembly that brought her to life. After forty-five minutes on the island, we boarded the ferry to Battery Park, hearts full and cameras richer.

Our bus picked us up for a late but satisfying Indian lunch at *Benares Tribeca*. Despite the crowd and the inconveniently located restrooms downstairs, the comforting meal of roti, rice, dal, vegetables, chicken, and curd revived us for the adventure ahead.

A Day Above the Skyline and Through the Heart of Manhattan

Next came the soaring experience of the *One World Observatory.* In just sixty seconds, the elevator swept us up to the 102nd floor, its walls alive with a digital animation tracing New York's evolving skyline.

At the top, a dramatic film ended with the screen lifting to reveal a breathtaking panorama: an instant gasp of skyline, rivers, bridges, and stories woven together. From the viewing deck, we enjoyed a full 360-degree vista of New York, New Jersey, Liberty Island, and the ferries moving toward Ellis Island. With delight, we even zoomed in to spot Neha's apartment and Abhishek's former apartment on the 70th floor.

We then reunited with our guide, a cheerful African American lady who proudly declared her love for Shah Rukh Khan, the Indian Bollywood star, before beginning our Manhattan city tour. At the 9/11 Memorial, her narration was deeply moving. She encouraged us to touch the water flowing into the reflecting pools, symbolizing the tears shed for the 2,977 lives lost that day. Nearby stood the Oculus, gleaming white and ribbed like wings of hope, surrounded by the new towers that have risen in quiet resilience.

We continued to *Rockefeller Center Plaza,* where the golden Prometheus statue stands watch. The sunken plaza transforms from a summer cafe into a winter skating rink, and a copper plaque marks the exact spot where the *city's tallest Christmas tree* is placed each year.

Our drive then took us past the United Nations Headquarters, Wall Street's *Charging Bull, and the Fearless Girl* standing bravely before it: a symbol of New York's relentless spirit.

We crossed the Garment District, glimpsed Apple's enormous store, the High Line, Little Island, grand hotels, theatres, stadiums, and even the Trump Building. Many corners of New York felt instantly familiar, as Neha and Abhishek had already shown us several of these places during our earlier visit.

Twilight in Neon: Losing and Finding Our Way in Times Square

As twilight deepened, we arrived at the pulsing heart of Manhattan: *Times Square*. Bathed in neon brilliance, the city glowed with an almost electric energy. We wandered through the lights, took photographs, and simply soaked in the spectacle.

At one point, we walked a little too far and somehow lost our way, despite moving in what felt like a straight line: a mystery later solved by Neha, who explained that many of the *"straight" roads in Times Square actually form triangles*. With shared locations and timely guidance from our tour manager, we rejoined the group just in time.

Before boarding the bus, Sunitha spotted some unusually large bananas at a nearby juice shop, priced at just one dollar each. We happily picked up a few; a delightfully simple pleasure amid Manhattan's dazzling chaos.

After dinner at a lovely Indian restaurant, we headed back to our hotel in Parsippany. By then, we had walked nearly 14,000 steps. A short stroll outside, a call to Neha and Abhishek to recount the day's adventures, especially our little *"lost and found"* episode, and soon we drifted into a deep, contented sleep. As the day ended, one truth lingered clearly in our minds: no city moves quite like New York, and no beginning to our 18-day journey could have been more perfect.

Day 3: Washington, D.C. – The Nation's Voice

"History whispers here, not in silence, but with pride."

We checked out of our hotel after breakfast the next morning and set off from New York on a scenic five-hour drive to our next destination: *Washington, D.C.*, where marble monuments and memorials echo the nation's past.

The bus departed at 9 a.m., but within an hour, heavy rain set in and continued throughout the day. As a result, much of our sightseeing was either from the bus or under umbrellas. Despite the downpour, the journey remained relaxed and picturesque, offering glimpses of charming landscapes along the way. We stopped en route for lunch at *Golden Corral*, an American buffet that proved to be a feast for the senses.

The restaurant had three huge counters: the first was filled with delicious desserts and cone ice creams in three flavours, all clearly labelled. The second featured Mexican dishes with tortillas and various fillings, pizza, roasted and fried chicken, multiple varieties of rice, noodles, breads, fresh and canned fruits, boiled broccoli, baked beans, corn, and potato wedges. The third counter offered five to six ready-to-eat salads, including coleslaw and Caesar, as well as ingredients to create your own salad. At a separate station, a staff member served soft drinks like Sprite and Coca-Cola, along with coffee and hot water.

I indulged moderately, choosing a little of everything: two kinds of chicken, tender lamb, a soft bun, fresh fruits, two salads, and a Coke. By the time I sat down, I already felt full, overwhelmed not by quantity but by the sheer variety before us.

Where Dreams Take Flight: From the Wright Brothers to the Stars

Our first stop after lunch was the *Smithsonian National Air and Space Museum*, a place where dreams quite literally take flight. The rain continued, and since our entry time was 4 p.m., we waited outside in a light drizzle for about thirty minutes before being allowed in.

Once inside, we were instantly awestruck. The exhibits spanned from the *Wright Brothers'* handmade planes to spacecraft bound for Mars. We wandered among fragile early aircraft, the Apollo moon capsule, and satellites that had once touched the stars. Models of fighter jets and rockets ignited our imagination at every turn.

We explored the cockpit of a Boeing and experienced a simulation of take-off and landing. We even touched a space rock: small but surprisingly heavy; and learned fascinating facts about black holes. The museum also featured several satellites, short films about missions to Pluto, and a few beautifully preserved vintage cars. Although the main rockets and space mission section was closed for renovation, we could still glimpse satellites and rockets from the escalators as we moved between floors.

America's Capital Unfolds: Landmarks, Legacies, and a Rainbow Farewell

The afternoon continued with our guided city tour, beginning at the *White House*: the official residence and workplace of the *President of the United States*. Seeing it in person felt almost surreal, as though a familiar image had stepped out of textbooks and television screens into real life. We eagerly captured photographs and cheerful selfies, quietly proud to stand before such an enduring symbol of American democracy.

As we moved through the city, *Washington, D.C.*, gradually revealed its layers of history and significance. Our guide, Ms. Felida, explained that the city, named after the first President, George Washington, is not a state but a unique federal district: the *District of Columbia*. She went on to describe the United States as a vast tapestry of governance: fifty states woven together with one federal district, five territories, and a scattering of distant islands.

She also shared an intriguing detail that caught our attention: by law, no building in the city is permitted to stand taller than the *Capitol*. Suddenly, the city's low, open skyline made perfect sense. Here, history is allowed to breathe without being overshadowed by steel and glass. Drones, too, are banned in the area, preserving the dignity and calm of this political heartland.

We passed through the famed *Embassy Row*, where the flags of 183 nations fluttered in harmonious rows, adding a vibrant international flavour to the city. Though modest in size, Washington, D.C., clearly stands at the crossroads of the world.

Our next stop was the *Jefferson Memorial*, followed by the majestic *Washington Monument*, a 555-foot marble obelisk whose reflection shimmered gently across the Reflecting Pool. Nearby stood the *International Trade Center*, developed during President Ronald Reagan's administration; a reminder that even in a historic city, modern chapters continue to unfold.

The rain drifted in and out, but the city's beauty remained serene beneath the grey sky. At the *Capitol Building*, home to the U.S. Senate and Congress, our guide paused the bus despite the drizzle, allowing us to step out for photographs and a closer look. Gazing up at its grand dome, the city felt like a living museum: every building a storyteller, every monument a chapter in America's long narrative.

As we continued, we passed the National Museum of the American Indian, honouring Indigenous communities first encountered by Columbus; the National Gallery of Art, whose architecture creates a striking four-dimensional optical illusion; and the Smithsonian Museum of Natural History, home to the legendary Hope Diamond from India. Nearby stood the National Museum of American History, where the elegant inaugural gowns of the First Ladies are displayed, tracing a graceful timeline of changing styles and legacies.

Our guide reminded us that all museums in Washington, D.C., are government-owned and free to visit. They line both sides of the National Mall: not a shopping mall, but a long, green cultural corridor filled with monuments, museums, gardens, and memories.

We concluded our city tour at the *Lincoln Memorial*, overlooking a tranquil reflecting pool with the Washington Monument rising proudly beyond it. Just as we prepared to leave, a soft drizzle returned. Then, as though nature had planned its own finale, a rainbow arched gracefully across the sky, framing the monument in vivid colours. It was a breathtaking sight: an unexpected tribute painted across the heavens. We captured the moment with delight, preserving it forever in our cameras.

From there, we drove toward our hotel near the Virginia state line, in the quiet town of Manassas, whose modest population lends it a calm, small-town charm. En route, we stopped for dinner at an Indian restaurant, *Banaras Express*. Since it was a Wednesday, Sunitha and I enjoyed chicken dry and mutton gravy with roti, along with samosa, jeera rice, dal, and curd; dessert was a warm and comforting gulab jamun. After a long, rain-soaked day, the familiar flavours felt deeply reassuring.

We finally reached the *Wyndham Garden Manassas* and checked into Room 514 on the fifth floor. The room was spacious and comfortable, with a double bed, a cosy sofa set, a work table, a coffee maker, a microwave, and a television. The bathroom was simple and functional. After unpacking and freshening up, we spoke to Neha and then settled in for the night: grateful for the warmth, rest, and memories of a day steeped in history and gentle wonder.

Day4: Hershey, Pennsylvania: A Town That Smells Like Chocolate

"Happiness is sweet, especially when it melts in your mouth."

We left our hotel after breakfast in a brand-new bus at 9 a.m., heading toward *Hershey, Pennsylvania:* a town that quite literally smells like chocolate. The three-hour countryside drive was scenic and relaxing, but the moment we arrived at the Hershey Chocolate Factory, excitement filled the air. It felt like stepping into a storybook world of cocoa and candy.

A Delicious Detour: Tracing Chocolate's Journey from Bean to Bar

The air grew sweeter the instant we entered *Hershey's Chocolate World*. The factory tour a continuous dark ride where we hop in a themed car blended learning with delight: machines hummed, chocolate flowed like liquid velvet, and the warm scent of cocoa wrapped around us.

The journey carried us through the entire chocolate-making process: from the harvesting, washing, drying, and fermenting of cocoa beans to their crushing and blending into cocoa liquor.

Hershey's uses a unique technique in which fresh milk is condensed and mixed with sugar; we watched in awe as this mixture was blended with cocoa liquor, transforming slowly into rich, creamy chocolate. The fully automated production line: from mixing to shaping to packaging, unfolded before us like a mesmerizing ballet of machines and sweetness.

At the end of the ride, we were greeted with a Hershey's chocolate sample and discount coupons for the factory store. The chocolates were warm, velvety, and irresistible.

We then wandered into the store for a bit of shopping. After picking up a few packets of Hershey's dark chocolate, we discovered a delightful surprise: self-dispensing stations filled with bite-sized varieties such as Kisses, Reese's, Almonds, Nuggets, and many more. Visitors could fill pouches or containers to the brim for a fixed price.

Naturally, we filled two pouches with every variety we could find, laughing like children in a candy wonderland. Using our discount coupons, we packed several more chocolates to take home: joy wrapped in foil, childhood reborn. We made sure to select some special ones for Neha and Abhishek before stepping out with hearts and hands full of chocolate treasures. It was truly a delicious detour; one that left us smiling long after we departed from the sweetest town in America.

Onward to Niagara Falls

After our visit to Hershey's, we boarded the bus and began the long journey toward *Niagara Falls.* Along the way, we stopped for lunch at an Indian restaurant called *Bollywood Fusion.* It was a self-service buffet, but the space was so cramped that even moving between the counters felt uncomfortable. One of the vegetable curries was overly salty, though the remaining dishes were acceptable.

The menu was limited, so none of us opted for a second helping. I ate a little onion pakora, some dal, cabbage curry, a small ladle of rice, a pappad, two quarter pieces of naan, a spoon of chicken gravy, and a cup of curd. With lunch completed, we resumed our drive and eventually reached Hyatt Place, our hotel near the iconic Niagara Falls.

Days 5–6: Niagara: Where Water Roars and Mist Dances

"The roar of the falls drowns out the world and awakens something within."

We reached *Niagara* around 8 p.m. and headed straight on foot to a restaurant called *The Buffet* for dinner. It was a simple but satisfying meal; meatballs, chicken, roti, dal, rice, and ice cream to end on a sweet note. Afterward, we proceeded to our hotel, *Hyatt Place Niagara*, and checked into Room 303.

The moment we walked in, the view took our breath away. From our window, we could see the American Falls, the Canadian skyline, the glowing Ferris wheel, and the ethereal mist drifting upward, softly lit by distant lights. It felt like stepping into a postcard come alive. After a quick round of unpacking and safely transferring our precious Hershey chocolates into the fridge, we stepped out just in time for the 10 p.m. fireworks.

Where Mist Meets Moonlight: Our First Night at the Falls

Right at 10 p.m., fireworks burst into life on the Canadian side, painting the sky with brilliant colours for a full five minutes. Their reflections glistening through the drifting mist, tinting it in shades of red, green, and gold. It felt magical; as though the night itself was celebrating.

A short five-minute stroll from our hotel brought us to the edge of *Niagara Falls,* where we stood absolutely awestruck. Few sights on earth can compare. The thunderous roar reverberated through our chests, and the cool spray brushed against our faces like a veil of silk.

What a spectacle it was: the illuminated skyline of Ontario glowing across the river, with the majestic Horseshoe Falls roaring beyond. On the U.S. side, we watched the furious rush of the Niagara River as it raced toward the brink, ready to plunge into thunder and mist. Nature, in its purest form, demanded our silence and admiration.

Exhausted after a long day of travel, we returned to our room, freshened up, and finally went to bed around 1:00 a.m. The day had drained our energy but filled our hearts; every moment was unforgettable.

A Dance with the Falls: From Maid of the Mist to the Hurricane Deck

The next morning, after breakfast, we made our way down to Niagara Falls to collect our tickets for the day's adventure. Excitement surged as we donned our blue raincoats for the legendary *Maid of the Mist cruise.*

An elevator whisked us 200 feet down in just 30 seconds, and soon we were aboard the *Blue Maid of the mist Boat*, the roar of the falls growing louder with every passing moment as we headed straight into history and the misty heart of Niagara.

Following Neha's advice, we positioned ourselves right at the front rail of the upper deck for the best view. As the boat set off, the air filled with thunder and spray. At first, the *American Falls and Bridal Veil Falls* appeared close and magnificent.

But as we approached the mighty *Horseshoe Falls*, the experience became exhilaratingly intense: the boat seemed to plunge straight into the cascading water, the roar deafening, the spray soaking us instantly, and the world dissolving into white water and wonder.

The spray drenched us completely; we laughed, shouted, and gasped, struggling to catch our breath through the exhilaration. Somehow, I managed to capture a few precious seconds of video while bracing myself against the wind.

Across the torrent, we spotted the *Canadian Maid of the Mist*, its boat *painted red*, passengers waving back in matching raincoats. For a brief, magical moment, the border vanished; replaced by shared joy and awe.

After the boat ride, we explored the riverbanks, strolling over bridges as the Niagara River rushed below in full fury: wild, untamed, and magnificent. Lunch followed at *Bombay Palace*, another comforting Indian restaurant.

In the afternoon, our adventure continued at the *Cave of the Winds*. A swift 30-second elevator ride carried us 193 feet down, where bright yellow raincoats awaited. We slipped them on and climbed a series of wooden decks that brought us astonishingly close to the roaring *Bridal Veil Falls,* with thunderous water crashing just a few feet away.

At the final platform, aptly named the *Hurricane Deck*, the force of the water was so powerful that we had to turn our backs to it, laughing through the spray as it drenched us from head to toe. Cameras fogged, and my reading glasses blurred completely in the mist, but our spirits soared, lifted by the raw, untamed energy of the falls.

All around us, seagulls circled and nested on the rocky embankments near the rushing water, their chicks huddled close by. I even noticed tiny snakes slipping between the stones; a quiet reminder of how vibrant and alive the natural world is around this elemental wonder. The roar of the falls, the wind whipping past, and the cool mist on our faces made us feel both impossibly small and infinitely alive.

Drenched from head to toe, we returned to the hotel. Both Suni and I felt uncomfortable, so we stepped off the bus and headed straight to our room. We removed our soaked clothes and shoes, took a quick wash, and slipped into dry, warm clothing. Exhaustion finally caught up with us, and we drifted into a much-needed half-hour nap.

Feeling refreshed, we later went down to the lobby, lacing up dry socks and shoes, before joining the group for dinner. Once again, we walked to *The Buffet*, the same Indian restaurant we had visited the previous night. The spread was similar: I enjoyed chicken biryani, chicken gravy, roti, and a little rice. I also tried the custard, though it was not particularly impressive. After dinner, we walked back to the hotel under the cool night air. Many in our group went shopping, but we preferred to return to our room and rest, letting the day's exhilaration gently settle.

From our window, we watched the Falls come alive in shifting hues of pink, blue, and gold: a breathtaking dance of water, light, and sound. No camera could ever capture its full majesty. Later, the nightly fireworks began, and we enjoyed the spectacle right from our window. Brilliant colours burst above the mist one last time; a perfect farewell to this magical destination.

That night, as we packed for our flight from the East Coast to Los Angeles, we fell asleep to the distant thunder of the falls, its steady rhythm echoing in our hearts like a gentle lullaby from one of nature's greatest wonders.

Farewell to Niagara

Bidding farewell to unforgettable Niagara Falls, we carried its mist and magic in our hearts as we made our way to *Buffalo Airport* at dawn. After check-in, we boarded Southwest Airlines for our flight to *Phoenix*, with a connecting flight onward to *Los Angeles*.

The journey across the continent was long but captivating, with America unfolding beneath us: from the misty landscapes of the East to the golden expanses of the West.

As the thunderous roar of Niagara faded beneath the clouds, our excitement turned westward, toward a city where dreams wear sunglasses and every corner holds a story. We landed in Phoenix around 12:30 p.m., adjusting our watches to the new three-hour time difference. After a brief layover, we continued on to Los Angeles, ready to embrace the next chapter of our adventure.

Days 7–8: Los Angeles - Lights, Camera, Reality

"In Los Angeles, every sunset feels like a curtain call and every street hides a story."

Our introduction to *Los Angeles* began the moment we stepped out of the airport and boarded our tour bus. After a long flight across the continent, our first stop was a comforting one: lunch at *Mayura*, a legendary South Indian restaurant run by Ms. Padmini and her husband for over two decades.

The meal was exceptional: authentic South Indian flavours with a gentle touch of Kerala. Fluffy rice, soft appam, crisp onion pakoras, mixed vegetable curry, cabbage fry, sambar, rasam, and a beautifully spiced fish gravy filled our plates. Mor kulambu, crunchy pappad, and a warm bowl of payasam completed the feast. Each dish tasted like home: the kind of food a mother prepares with love. To find such authenticity in the U.S. felt almost unbelievable.

From Sunset Strip to Starlit Skies: Los Angeles Unveiled

With hearts satisfied and stomachs full, we set off on our guided city tour. We drove past *Sunset Strip*, the Rainbow Bar and Grill, and iconic restaurants and comedy clubs that had once hosted Hollywood's brightest stars. Soon, the stately *Los Angeles City Hall* came into view: a historic building that had once served as a fire station and now houses the registration offices for both Los Angeles and Beverly Hills. Further ahead stretched the sunlit coastline of Santa Monica and Malibu, where the legendary *Baywatch* series was filmed.

Our guide filled the journey with fascinating snippets of history: California was once part of Mexico, and its cultural influence still runs deep. She also reminded us that Los Angeles lies in an earthquake-prone zone, explaining the predominance of low-rise homes and quake-resistant structures.

Our next stop was the glamorous enclave of *Beverly Hills*, where luxurious mansions of film stars and musicians hide behind tall hedges, fiercely guarding their privacy. We paused for photos at the iconic *Beverly Hills sign*, an emblem of cinematic glamour seen in countless movies. From there, the tour carried us to the *Dolby Theatre*, home of the world-famous Academy Awards. Riding up the grand escalators, we caught our first clear glimpse of the *Hollywood Sign* standing proudly atop the hills. Originally erected by a real-estate developer as an illuminated wooden advertisement, it later gained global fame, appearing in films and attracting visitors from around the world, eventually being rebuilt in steel.

Hollywood Boulevard buzzed with energy as we walked along the *Walk of Fame*. More than 2,700 stars glistening beneath our feet, honouring legends of film, music, and television. We also stopped by the *TCL Chinese Theatre*, famous for its forecourt of celebrity hand-and footprints; timeless impressions of greatness. The street throbbed with life: tourists clicking photos, street performers entertaining the crowd, and vendors lining the sidewalks. There was also increased police presence due to a peaceful protest by the LGBTQIA community, adding to the city's ever-unpredictable rhythm.

As evening settled over the city, we drove up to the *Griffith Observatory*, perched high above Los Angeles. Inside, we explored telescopes, captivating exhibits on space, and intricate models of planets and galaxies. Stepping out onto the terrace, we witnessed one of the most spectacular sights of our journey: the city of Los Angeles glowing endlessly under the night sky, a shimmering galaxy of its own.

Dinner awaited us at *Indian Tandoori*, where a warm Punjabi buffet brought the day to a comforting close: dal makhni, paneer dishes, rice, rotis, lamb gravy, chicken, and sweet gulab jamuns.

Exhausted from travel, time-zone changes, and a full day of sightseeing, we finally checked into *Holiday Inn at La Mirada*. Room 444 became our sanctuary for the night. We unpacked, freshened up, and drifted into sleep, letting the glow of Los Angeles fade gently into dreams. After such a long and exhausting day, we were too tired even to call Neha.

A Cinematic Odyssey Through Universal Studios Hollywood Thrills, Magic, and Unforgettable Family Moments

After breakfast, we boarded the bus at 9 a.m. for *Universal Studios Hollywood* and reached the park by 10 a.m. Our tour guide handed us all-access ride tickets, and since lunch wasn't included, he gave Sunitha and me twenty dollars each. Neha had already briefed us on what to see and even shown us videos, and our guide added his own suggestions, so we felt well prepared for the day ahead.

The Legendary Studio Tour

Our first stop was the famous *Studio Tour on the Upper Lot.* We boarded the tram: a long, open train, while the onboard guide narrated each highlight as we rolled through the backlot.

We witnessed several live effects and iconic movie sets: mechanical sharks lunging from the water, sudden bursts of fire, and the dramatic recreation of an underground subway station during a powerful *"earthquake."* The shaking tram and collapsing structures felt uncannily real. Moments later, we entered another zone where lightning cracked, rain poured, and a massive *flash flood* surged toward us: an exhilarating spectacle.

Throughout the one-hour tour, we passed sets from well-known films and television shows, with the guide sharing fascinating behind-the-scenes stories at every turn. It was thrilling, immersive, and absolutely unforgettable experience.

After the Studio Tour, we walked toward the Water World show area. The staff at Universal Studios were exceptionally courteous and helpful, always guiding visitors with a smile. We were informed that the first show would begin only at 2:30 p.m., so with time to spare, we decided to return later.

Harry Potter's Magical World

Next, we crossed into the spellbinding realm of the *Wizarding World of Harry Potter*, marked by a towering castle and beautifully themed pathways. Our first adventure here was the *Forbidden Journey* ride inside Hogwarts Castle. Although the wait time was nearly fifty minutes, we joined the queue: after all, Neha had insisted it was an absolute must, especially for her, a die-hard Harry Potter fan. The single-rider line is always shorter, but Sunitha and I wanted to experience every ride together.

The 3D ride was spectacular. We soared through Quidditch fields, dodged dragons, and whirled through castle towers, laughing and screaming in delight as we followed Harry on a magical chase, just like in the movies. It was truly exhilarating.

Next came *Flight of the Hippogriff*, a fast and twisting roller coaster with a forty-five-minute wait. After nearly a decade away from roller coasters, the thrill was worth every second: plunging one way and whipping around the other, leaving us laughing breathlessly.

Afterward, we stopped at a cart to try the famous *Butterbeer* that Neha had insisted we taste. It was rich, creamy, and delicious. Sunitha took just a sip, while I happily finished the entire cup.

We then joined a short queue for a small Harry Potter magic show in a room filled with wands. It wasn't particularly impressive for us, but younger children and devoted fans would likely enjoy it much more.

Descent to the Lower Lot

To reach the *Lower Lot*, we took three massive escalators that carried us deep down the hillside. Along the way, we passed an enormous construction site: the groundwork for what will soon become the world's longest roller coaster, an exciting future addition to the park.

Our first stop was *Revenge of the Mummy*. The forty-five-minute wait proved worthwhile. The ride was pure adrenaline: sudden jet-speed launches, abrupt stops, high-speed reverses, and terrifying encounters with beetles and mummies. We emerged breathless, wide-eyed, and laughing. The *Transformers* 3D attraction was unfortunately closed, but a giant Transformer replica outside more than made up for it. We took photos from several angles.

Next came *Mario Kart: Bowser's Challenge*, an interactive VR ride where each of us wore a headset synced with 3D glasses. Racing through vibrant digital tracks, we fired at targets to score points. A hundred points would win a prize; we proudly finished with seventy-eight, which felt like a victory in itself.

We considered *Jurassic World-The Ride*, but after watching riders emerge completely drenched from the final drop, we decided against it. After being soaked at Niagara Falls during the Maid of the Mist, we weren't ready for another cold drenching.

Lunch and the Return to the Upper Lot

By 2 p.m., hunger struck. Unable to find suitable food stalls, we called Neha, who quickly located online a nearby Chinese kitchen: *Panda Express*. Their Orange Chicken and Teriyaki Chicken combo, served with fried rice, noodles, and a fortune cookie, was delicious and satisfying.

With the Lower Lot covered, we rode back up the three giant escalators to the Upper Lot. We hoped to catch the Water World show, but arrived just five minutes after the gates had closed. The next show was scheduled for 5:45 p.m., but our tour manager had instructed everyone to assemble at the Universal Globe by 6 p.m., so we reluctantly had to skip it.

Upper Lot Adventures

With time still on hand, we explored more attractions. *Minion Mayhem* was a lively 3D ride through Gru's laboratory, filled with laughter and chaos. *Silly Swirly* stirred memories of taking Neha to amusement parks when she was little. The *Kung Fu Panda Adventure* was a cheerful 3D show aimed mainly at children, but enjoyable nonetheless.

We paused to watch children and adults playing in the water zone, splashing and shrieking with joy. Although we considered repeating the Studio Tour, the timing didn't work: a fifteen-minute wait plus the hour-long ride would have made us late. Instead, we strolled through the park, taking photographs, soaking in the atmosphere, and letting the day's excitement settle.

By 6 p.m., we gathered near the iconic Universal Studios Globe, tired, happy, and overflowing with memories. As our bus drove away, the lights of Los Angeles twinkled beneath the evening sky, as if Hollywood itself were winking at us.

Dinner awaited us once again at *Indian Tandoori*, familiar flavours after a day of fantasy and thrills. Surprisingly, despite so much walking, our step count was only 8,000: thanks to the long wait times at the rides.

Back at the hotel, we freshened up and spoke to Neha and Abhishek, excitedly recounting the day's adventures.

Sleep came quickly that night. Universal Studios had gifted us a day filled with magic, thrills, and childlike joy: a cinematic odyssey we knew we would cherish forever.

Days 9–10: Las Vegas and Beyond: From Neon Horizons to Timeless Canyons

"Between sand and neon, Las Vegas glows with the promise of nights that outshine the day."

Anniversary in the City of Lights: Las Vegas Unfolded

It was our *wedding anniversary today*: thirty-four years of togetherness. I wished Sunitha as soon as I woke up. We got ready early, packed our bags by 9 a.m., and boarded the bus from *Los Angeles to Las Vegas*. From coastal calm to desert dazzle, Las Vegas felt like stepping into an entirely different universe.

The road to Vegas stretched through vast expanses of arid land, rugged mountains, and endless rows of solar farms glimmering under the desert sun. Our guide explained that the region's harsh climate made solar energy a major power source, especially as water levels at the Hoover Dam continue to decline.

The journey itself was lively. Everyone on the bus took turns singing, and when my turn came, I shared that we were celebrating our thirty-fourth wedding anniversary. The group cheered and wished us warmly.

I then sang an English adaptation of a Mohammed Rafi classic: *"The she I love is a beautiful, beautiful dream come true..."* Sunitha, too, sang two songs on request. It became a joyful celebration on wheels: a memorable beginning to a special day.

We stopped for lunch at *India Palace* in Las Vegas before checking into our hotel: the *Luxor Hotel and Casino*, an enormous pyramid-shaped structure with a laser beam shooting from its tip, said to be visible even from space.

The hotel was awe-inspiring, rising thirty floors and housing nearly 4,400 rooms. Its three colour-coded zones: Green, Blue, and Red, guided guests to the appropriate elevator banks. Our room was in the Green Zone, Room 484.

Inside, the Luxor felt like a world unto itself, with an endless expanse of gaming tables, slot machines, blackjack counters, horse-racing simulators, and every kind of casino entertainment imaginable. It truly felt like stepping into a city within a city.

The Luxor is part of the MGM group, along with its two neighbouring properties: *Mandalay Bay,* famous for its impressive shark aquarium, and *Excalibur,* designed like a vibrant medieval castle. The three hotels are connected by a free shuttle bus, a convenient monorail, and even underground walkways, making it easy to explore this dazzling entertainment hub.

Later in the afternoon, we set off on a guided city tour. Our guide shared that Las Vegas has around three million residents and welcomes over four million visitors annually. Most people work in driving, food services, casinos, or the wedding industry. We learnt that the temperatures here soar between 43°C and 47°C from June to September, and no tree grows naturally here: every single one is transplanted.

Each casino has its own independent water and power source, separate from the city grid, with much of the electricity generated through solar energy.

Our first stop was the iconic *"Welcome to Fabulous Las Vegas"* sign, where we clicked several photos to mark the moment. We then drove along the legendary *Las Vegas Strip*, where each hotel and casino is a world of its own: *The Flamingo, the Bellagio, Caesars Palace, New York–New York* with its miniature Statue of Liberty, *Paris* with its replica Eiffel Tower, and the gleaming golden *Trump Tower*. Each property tells a story through light and architecture.

At the *Bellagio Fountains*, we watched a breathtaking five-minute show at dusk, with water, music, and lights perfectly synchronized. Millions of lights danced in harmony, drawing gasps from the crowd. Further down the Strip, our guide pointed out *The Sphere*, a newly built spherical entertainment arena near *The Venetian*, visible from across the city with its ever-changing digital displays and a world within it.

We also saw *Harry Reid International Airport*, the fifth busiest in the United States, with one take-off or landing every thirty seconds. The guide explained how Elvis Presley helped make Las Vegas world-famous. He lived and performed here and even got married in the city, which is now known as the

Wedding Capital of the World: where one can register today and get married tomorrow, and, as our guide joked, get divorced just as easily.

Our next stop was *Fremont Street*, the oldest part of Las Vegas, established in 1905. *"Vegas" means "grass,"* and our guide recounted how this area once belonged to a mob-run town before transforming into a casino hub. Today, Fremont Street is an explosion of light and sound: five blocks long, lined with ten casinos, and covered by a massive digital canopy stretching over 2.5 blocks. Street performers, musicians, acrobats, and costumed characters filled the space. Photos with them were readily available: for a small fee, of course. Forty-five minutes felt like five; it was over far too soon.

We ended the evening with dinner once again at *India Palace*. Afterward, three other couples from our tour group decided to join us for a night adventure through Las Vegas. The night was still young, and we all agreed it was a once-in-a-lifetime experience not to be missed. We bought tickets for the Deuce Double-Decker Bus: a 24-hour pass costing just $8, operating like a hop-on, hop-off service along the Strip.

Climbing to the top deck, we found seats right at the front and watched in awe as the city came alive below us: a dazzling ribbon of colour, energy, and dreams stretching endlessly through the desert night. After a couple of hours cruising through the neon-lit city, we got down at the southern end, crossed the road, and boarded the return bus back to our hotel. The view was mesmerizing. Las Vegas truly lives up to its name: *the desert in neon.*

The Grand Canyon and Hoover Dam: Earth's Masterpiece

"Where earth meets sky, the Grand Canyon and Hoover Dam remind us how small we are and how vast the world can be."

The next morning, we temporarily left behind the neon glow of Las Vegas, and the landscape transformed almost immediately. The vast desert stretched before us, quiet and timeless. Soon, we felt we were approaching the meeting point of nature's grandeur and human ingenuity: the Grand Canyon and the Hoover Dam: two masterpieces that reflect the delicate balance between ambition and the enduring power of the Earth.

We departed by bus at 9:00 a.m. for a three-hour drive to the world-famous *Grand Canyon* in *Arizona*. This natural wonder stretches 277 miles in length, spans up to 29 kilometres in width, and plunges nearly 6,000 feet down to the Colorado River flowing far below. Upon arrival, we learned that visitors must take a free shuttle bus to reach Eagle Point, the first viewing area and home to the famous Skywalk. After collecting our tickets from our manager, we boarded the shuttle and entered the park.

Nothing could have prepared us for the sheer grandeur of the canyon. Vast stretches of rock unfolded before us, painted in layers of red, brown, and gold, sculpted patiently by time itself. At *Eagle Point,* the natural rock formations resembled *a majestic eagle with its wings spread wide*: a breathtaking sight that left us spellbound.

Next, we made our way to the *Skywalk*, a remarkable glass bridge suspended 4,000 feet above the canyon floor: a true marvel of modern engineering. Though I had imagined it would be terrifying to step onto transparent glass hanging over such a vast void, the experience was surprisingly calm and almost magical.

Visitors are allowed fifteen minutes on the Skywalk, but those opting for the official photographer are permitted to stay a little longer. We gladly chose that option, lingering to soak in the views and capture the moment. The professional photographs turned out beautifully. We selected one favourite image and later downloaded it through their app for $26: worth every dollar for the memory, it preserved.

After our Skywalk experience, we headed to the Rooftop Restaurant, included in our ticket package, for lunch with a spectacular view. I enjoyed a chicken burger topped with American cheese, lettuce, tomato, red onion, dill pickle, and Skywalk sauce, accompanied by mac and cheese and an ice-cold Coke. Sunitha chose the spicy black bean veggie burger with mac and cheese and a diet Coke. The meal was delicious and deeply satisfying.

Post-lunch, we visited the Native Indian Village and Museum, where we saw tepees, traditional artifacts, and even met a Native American woman dressed in colourful attire. She graciously posed for a photo with us after a short prayer chant by a tribal singer. It was a serene, culturally enriching experience. We then boarded the bus and began our journey toward the Hoover Dam. Some members of our group opted for an additional helicopter-and-boat tour down to the canyon base: a thrilling adventure priced at $356 per person.

The *Hoover Dam*, an arch-gravity concrete structure spanning the Black Canyon of the *Colorado River*, stands on the border between Nevada and Arizona. Built between 1931 and 1936 during the Great Depression, it was officially dedicated on September 30, 1935, one year before its completion.

Even today, it remains a striking symbol of human determination and engineering excellence. Nearby, a newer arch bridge: part of Interstate 93, now carries traffic high above the dam. Opened in 2010, it added another impressive layer to the landscape. The entire setting was awe-inspiring, and we took plenty of photographs before beginning our return journey to Las Vegas.

Dinner that evening was at the *Gandhi Restaurant.* Later, back at the Luxor Hotel, we spent some time exploring the casino. It was my first experience gambling: I initially won $7, but soon lost $25. Still, the thrill was worth it.

Midnight Magic at the Bellagio

With the night still young, we stepped out once again and purchased tickets for the Deuce Double-Decker Bus. To our surprise, the fare was only $4 per person, as it was close to midnight. Our destination was the iconic *Bellagio Casino*, celebrated for its unmatched elegance and built at a staggering cost of $2.1 billion.

After a short ride, we got down opposite the Bellagio. Reaching the entrance required climbing five escalators to cross the busy street, each level revealing stunning views of nearby landmarks like *Paris Las Vegas* and the *Flamingo*.

Inside, the Bellagio was nothing short of breathtaking. We were greeted by an enormous indoor garden: a magical world of vibrant flowers, intricate sculptures, and larger-than-life creations shaped like animals and people. Every corner felt alive with colour and imagination. Elegant carpets, glittering chandeliers, and artistic floral installations enhanced the atmosphere of refined luxury. We stood awestruck, capturing every detail in countless photographs. Later, we took the Duece bus back to our hotel, Luxor, and called it a night; tired indeed, but deeply happy after a fabulous day filled with adventure and bliss.

The next morning, we checked out of the Luxor Hotel at 9 a.m. and boarded the bus. Our first stop was breakfast at the *Gandhi* Restaurant. After a hearty meal, we visited the *Eiffel Tower Casino Hotel.* Unfortunately, it opened only at 11:30 a.m., so we returned to the bus and instead headed to the Stratosphere Tower: one of Las Vegas's most famous landmarks and the tallest building in the city.

At the Stratosphere Tower, an elevator whisked us up to the 108th floor, unveiling a stunning 360-degree panorama of Las Vegas and its glittering skyline. We then ascended one level higher, to the 109th floor, where thrilling attractions like the Sky Jump awaited: both exciting and terrifying to witness.

After enjoying the views, we returned to the bus and stopped once more for lunch at India Palace Restaurant. Soon after, we drove to the airport to catch our Southwest Airlines flight to San Francisco, ready for the next chapter of our journey.

Days 11–12: San Francisco - Bridges, Memories, and the Light of Old Friendships

"San Francisco whispers its stories in fog and sunlight, where every bridge connects more than shores, it connects souls."

A Reunion After 45 Years - A Friendship Time Could Never Fade

The flight landed at *San Francisco International Airport* around 6 p.m., and to our delight, my schoolmate and close buddy Patanjali Bhat was waiting for us at the luggage carousel. We had planned to meet each other well in advance since our tour had a two-day halt in San Francisco, and he lived in the Bay Area, making it the perfect opportunity for a long-awaited reunion.

We had studied together at Kendriya Vidyalaya, Hebbal, in South Bangalore for several years and completed our 12th standard together in 1979: 45 years ago. Meeting him after more than four decades was an emotional and heartwarming moment. He greeted both Suni and me with a big hug and to my surprise, he still looked like the evergreen boy from our school days.

We collected our bags and followed him to his car. I had already informed our tour manager on the flight, that Sunitha and I would not be joining the tour group for dinner, and he kindly left our room keys at the hotel reception.

Pat then took us on a long drive around San Francisco, sharing stories about the Bay Area, his life over the last 45 years, and his beautiful family. The *Bay Area* was captivating, one side bathed in warm sunshine, the other shrouded in cool mist. He even drove us to the Pacific Ocean, where we stopped to admire the waves and the fading evening light.

We then went to his lovely home, which reflected his warmth and artistic spirit. Since our school days, Pat had been a talented musician and true to form, his living room had two pianos. He played a few soulful tunes for us, including one he had composed on friendship, in celebration of our reunion.

Pat also had two adorable *Goldendoodle dogs*, a lively six-month-old puppy, and a calm four-year-old companion. We met his gracious wife and son, shared a bottle of champagne, and reminisced about our school days, teachers, and old friends. His wife had prepared a delicious dinner, and the entire evening was filled with nostalgia, laughter, and warmth.

By the time we realized, it was already 12:30 a.m. Pat handed me a bottle of white wine as a parting gift, a touching gesture that I will always cherish. Sunitha couldn't help but marvel at how youthful he looked; indeed, his secret seemed to be an active lifestyle of fishing, sailing, trekking, marathon running, and, above all, a cheerful heart. We finally reached our hotel, *Hyatt Place Fremont, San Francisco*, where we collected our room keys, went up to our room, freshened up, and retired for the night.

It had been a truly unforgettable day, one filled with friendship, memories, and the joy of reconnecting across time.

Alcatraz Legends, Golden Gate Views, and Bay Reflections

Inside Alcatraz: Stories Etched in Stone and Silence

The next morning, we left by bus with our tour group at 8:30 a.m. for our visit to *Alcatraz Island.* We reached Pier 33 and boarded a cruise to the island. As we docked, our guide began explaining its history, how it became part of the U.S. National Park Service and an archaeological site, open today as a major tourist attraction.

Alcatraz, we learnt, was originally built by the U.S. Army to house deserters and military prisoners, before being converted into a high-security federal prison. Over the years, it held some of America's most notorious criminals, including *Al Capone, Machine Gun Kelly, and the Birdman of Alcatraz.* During our tour, we even saw Al Capone's prison cell: No. 113, an eerie reminder of the island's infamous past.

As we approached the island, a hand-painted sign caught my attention on the wall, it read: *"Indian Welcome-Indian Land."* Our guide explained that in 1969, a group of Native Americans occupied the island for 19 months, demanding recognition of their land rights. They refused to leave until it was officially declared a protected heritage site, a historic act that's remembered to this day.

Inside the prison, each of us received an audio-guide device that narrated stories in various languages; we chose English. The narration vividly described the daily routines of the inmates: their meal times, bath areas, and the small open yards where they were allowed brief moments of relaxation. The cells themselves were tiny and stark, furnished only with a narrow cot, a small table, and a toilet. Some isolation cells were even more disturbing, with double iron doors and no light at all, used for *solitary confinement.* Dark, silent, and chilling.

One cell stood out to me in particular; it displayed *beautiful paintings* created by an inmate whose artwork later found its way into galleries. It was a poignant reminder that even within the harsh confines of a prison cell, creativity could still find a way to bloom.

We walked through the entire complex, observing old mugs, blankets, and beds from that era, along with black-and-white photographs of the officers and famous prisoners who once lived there. After completing the tour and returning our audio devices, we boarded the cruise back to Pier 33, quietly reflecting on the haunting history we had just witnessed.

We then rejoined our bus and headed for lunch at a *North Indian Restaurant.* After lunch, our guided city tour of San Francisco began.

As we drove through the charming streets, our local guide pointed out the city's iconic landmarks: the elegant Victorian houses, the famously steep roads, and the historic cable cars that define San Francisco's character. We visited *Twin Peaks,* a pair of scenic hilltops that offer a sweeping panoramic view of downtown San Francisco, its striking skyline, and the sparkling Bay below. The view was simply breathtaking.

At the Golden Gate: Where Engineering Meets Eternity

Next, we stopped at the majestic *Golden Gate Bridge*, where the sunlight and mist played beautifully around the towering red arches, we took plenty of photographs to capture the moment. *San Francisco is a diverse, iconic, and historic city*. No visit to San Francisco is complete without witnessing the Golden Gate Bridge in all its splendour.

Standing at the viewpoint: the iconic red-orange towers rose gracefully against the blue waters of the bay, often shrouded in a mystical veil of fog. The panoramic view captures not only the bridge's engineering brilliance but also the timeless beauty of the surrounding hills and skyline.

Nearby, in the landscaped garden, we admired a detailed *steel working model* of the bridge. It offered visitors a fascinating glimpse into its intricate construction; an artistic tribute to the genius and grit that built this world-famous landmark.

Our next stop was the *San Francisco City Hall*, a majestic building where all official functions take place, from weddings to citizenship ceremonies. The gardens and trees surrounding it were beautifully maintained, making it another perfect photo spot.

Sailing the Bay - Under the Golden Gate's Mighty Span

By late afternoon, we reached Pier 43, where we boarded the famous Red and White Fleet *Princess* for our *Golden Gate Bay Cruise*. The sail offered a completely new perspective of the majestic Golden Gate Bridge, with the wind in our hair and the setting sun casting a soft golden glow across the Bay. Gliding beneath the bridge and looking up at its vast steel structure was truly awe-inspiring.

As our boat passed under its soaring span, we could fully appreciate the scale and grace of the giant bridge towering above us. The cool breeze carried the scent of the sea, and the rhythmic waves shimmered like liquid silver in the sunlight.

To our delight, we spotted several surfers balancing on handheld sailboards, their colourful sails catching the wind as they skimmed swiftly across the water; tiny but vivid figures dancing over the waves against the backdrop of the grand Golden Gate. It was a lively, unforgettable scene that beautifully captured the spirit of *San Francisco Bay*.

After the cruise, we rejoined our group and drove to *Curry Corner Restaurant* for dinner. Tired but content, we returned to our hotel after a day filled with beauty, history, and the unique magic of San Francisco. We spoke to Neha, described the wonderful day we had, wished her good night, and soon drifted into sleep.

"In San Francisco, every bridge spans more than water; it connects memories, friendships, and the quiet truths time cannot fade."

The next morning, as our bus rolled out of San Francisco, I looked back at the city that had given us so much in just two days: its misty bridges, its stories of resilience, and the warmth of friendships rekindled after decades.

From the haunting silence of Alcatraz to the grandeur of the Golden Gate and the quiet charm of its neighbourhoods, every corner of San Francisco had a story to tell. It was a city that blended history and heart, modern energy, and timeless grace.

With beautiful memories and hearts full of gratitude, we continued our journey toward the next chapter of our American adventure; onward to new horizons and experiences yet to unfold, with Orlando as our next destination.

Travel Day: From San Francisco to Orlando

We woke up very early that morning, as we had to check out of our hotel at 3:00 a.m. After collecting our packed breakfast: a simple meal of fruits, orange juice, and a bun, we boarded the bus to San Francisco International Airport. Our Southwest Airlines flight to *Chicago* was scheduled for 6 a.m., and though we were still half-asleep, there was a quiet excitement about moving from the cool, misty coast of California to the sunny heart of Florida. The flight from San Francisco to Chicago was smooth, and we landed around noon. After freshening up in the airport restrooms, we boarded our connecting flight to *Orlando*.

Our tour manager had given each of us $20 for lunch, but with the tight connection, there was barely time to grab anything. Thankfully, Sunitha had packed a few energy bars, which kept us going. During the flight, the airline staff served complimentary hot chocolate and salty pretzel twists; a small but very welcome treat.

Days 13–16: From the Golden Gate to the Sunshine State - Orlando, Florida

"Crossing coasts, we chased the sun, from California dreams to Florida magic."

We landed at *Orlando International Airport* around 5 p.m., excited yet weary after a full day of travel. After collecting our luggage, we boarded our tour bus, which drove us straight to dinner at a restaurant called *Taste of Punjab*. Having been awake since 3 a.m. and barely eaten anything all day, the delicious spread of Indian food felt heavenly. Everyone relished the hot rotis, curries, and desserts with great enthusiasm.

After dinner, we checked into our hotel, the *Crowne Plaza, Lake Buena Vista*, Orlando. The moment we entered our room, the soft bed and cozy interiors felt like a blessing. Exhausted but content, we freshened up and went to bed early, ready to recharge for three full days in Florida: the land of sunshine, theme parks, and childhood dreams.

Orlando: Where Magic Lives

The final leg of our journey had brought us to Florida, a state of endless sunshine and imagination. Our days in Orlando were filled with wonder. At Disney's Magic Kingdom, childhood dreams came alive beneath glittering fireworks and fairy-tale castles. Epcot carried us across worlds of innovation and global culture, while SeaWorld blended excitement with awe, dolphins dancing in sparkling fountains, giant killer whales leaping high, and penguins gliding across icy waters. Each park had its own heartbeat, and together they made Orlando a universe of laughter, wonder and unforgettable memories.

Day 1: A Day of Wonder at Epcot Center

Exploring the Future, the World, and a Sky of Fireworks

After a refreshing night's sleep at the Crowne Plaza, we went down for breakfast at 7:30 a.m. and left by bus at 8:30 a.m. for *Epcot Center*, one of the most fascinating parks at Walt Disney World.

Our tour manager handed each of us $60 as a lunch allowance for the next three days. We reached Epcot by 9:30 a.m., collected our tickets, and were instructed to regroup at the main gate at 6:30 p.m.

Following advice from both Neha and our tour manager, we planned our day well. We began with *Spaceship Earth*, the iconic silver dome that symbolizes Epcot, an immersive journey through human progress, from ancient communication to the digital era. Next came *Mission:* SPACE (Orange Mission), a thrilling simulation of a space launch. The powerful G-force, weightlessness, and our assigned roles: captain, navigator, pilot, and engineer, made it a fun, team-driven experience. After a brief orientation on what to do, we were divided into groups of four, Sunitha and I teamed up with two other visitors, ready to take on our mission.

But the true highlight was *Guardians of the Galaxy*: Cosmic Rewind, the fastest roller coaster we had ever been on. With dazzling visuals, rapid spins, and exhilarating twists, it had us screaming and laughing throughout. After that adrenaline rush, we slowed down with *Project Tomorrow*, followed by gentle boat rides such as *The Seas with Nemo* and *Journey of Water*. We also enjoyed *Living with the Land*, a calming cruise through futuristic greenhouses and sustainable farming displays.

By then, hunger struck. I enjoyed a roast chicken and cheese sandwich with pasta salad, while Sunitha chose a Mediterranean vegetable sandwich.

Post-lunch, we experienced *Soarin' Around the World*, a breathtaking flight simulator that whisked us across iconic global landmarks: the snow-capped Swiss Alps, the icy plains of Greenland, the vast coastlines of Australia, the charming landscapes of Germany, the majestic Great Wall of China, the timeless pyramids of Egypt, the vibrant colours of India's Taj Mahal, the sweeping plains of Tanzania, the elegance of France, and many more. It was magical, giving us the sensation of truly flying across the world in just a few unforgettable minutes.

In the afternoon, we explored the *World Showcase*, where pavilions represented different countries, each with its own architecture, food, and entertainment. We waited nearly 50 minutes for Remy's Ratatouille Adventure in the *France Pavilion*, an adorable ride that follows the little chef through a bustling French kitchen. It felt like a tiny roller-coaster experience, and the entire adventure was absolutely hilarious. From there, we wandered into the *Morocco Pavilion*, admiring its intricate tiles and desert-style courtyards. The *American Pavilion* came next, where we watched The American Dream, a 30-minute show that beautifully depicted the country's history through lifelike animatronic characters.

By 5 p.m., Sunitha and I decided to stay back to see more of Epcot and enjoy the famous nighttime fireworks show. I informed our tour manager and two other families from our group about our plan. One couple, Ravi and his wife decided to join us.

Together, the four of us continued exploring. We revisited Morocco as they had not seen it, then moved on to Japan, where we were captivated by traditional drumming performances. The *Germany Pavilion* charmed us with its fairy-tale buildings, followed by *Italy*, and then *China,* where we enjoyed a spectacular show about the country's heritage. In *Norway*, we took the ch Frozen boat ride, and in *Mexico*, we ended our circuit with a cheerful Donald Duck boat adventure.

As evening fell, we picked up some takeaway food, noodles and momos from the China Pavilion and found a perfect spot near the lagoon to watch the fireworks. Ravi and I grabbed a couple of beers, and just as we returned, the *fireworks* began. For fifteen minutes, the night sky lit up with colours and music, a mesmerizing spectacle that left us spellbound.

After the show, we strolled back slowly, taking a few more photos under the glowing lights of Epcot. We booked a cab from the entrance of Epcot to our hotel; the fare was $44, which we split, and we added a $5 tip. We reached late, freshened up, and fell asleep almost instantly, tired but filled with joy after one of the most extraordinary days of our trip.

A perfect blend of science, culture, and magic, Epcot left us enchanted.

Day 2: A Magical Day at Magic Kingdom

Fairytales, Friendship, and Fond Memories

After breakfast at our hotel, we left by bus at 8:30 a.m. for *Magic Kingdom*, the most iconic of all Disney parks. We reached by 9:30 a.m., and just like the previous day, our tour manager handed us our full-day passes.

To enter the park, we took the *Monorail*, gliding smoothly over the lake toward the castle gates. The other option was the *ferry*, which we decided to try on our return journey. Inside the park, a charming steam-engine train circled the grounds, stopping at different themed areas, free for all visitors. We boarded the train and got off at *Adventureland*, ready to begin our day of fun.

Our first thrill was the *Seven Dwarfs Mine Train*, a delightful roller coaster that whisked us through sparkling caves and scenes from Snow White's fairytale world. Next came *Under the Sea*: Journey of the Little Mermaid, a gentle boat ride that told Ariel's story with enchanting songs and colourful underwater scenes. Then we tried The *Barnstormer*, a kiddie roller coaster that turned out to be surprisingly enjoyable even for adults. Nearby, we watched a lively *Circus Parade*, where Sunitha happily posed for a picture with a smiling lady on stilts.

With a map in hand, we made our way toward *Fantasyland and Tomorrowland*, both nearby and easily walkable. At Fantasyland, our first stop was Buzz Lightyear's *Space Ranger*

Spin, an interactive space-themed game where we fired laser guns at targets to earn points while our two-seater cars spun in all directions. It was great fun.

We then boarded the *People Mover*, an elevated 10-minute train ride that offered a relaxing tour of Tomorrowland's futuristic attractions. After that came the nostalgic *Carousel of Progress*, a slow-turning ride that showcased how daily life has evolved through the decades, a trip down memory lane.

Being a Sunday, the park was crowded, and by lunchtime, we were starving. We stopped for chicken burgers loaded with lettuce, tomato, onion, and dill pickle, washed down with chilled Coke. Simple but satisfying. After lunch, we strolled toward *Liberty Square* just as the *grand parade* was about to begin. We even managed to find seats, but at the last minute, we decided to hop onto the Liberty Belle Riverboat, moored right across from where we had been sitting. As the riverboat set sail, we could see the parade had already started, and we just managed a glimpse of the first few floats and dancers. Poor Sunitha was quite disappointed to have missed it.

The *Liberty Belle Riverboat* was a charming journey back in time, gliding smoothly along the scenic Rivers of America in the heart of Magic Kingdom. Aboard the grand, white, three-tiered paddle steamer, we enjoyed a 20-minute leisurely ride surrounded by lush greenery, rustic frontier scenes, and glimpses of iconic attractions along the riverbank. The gentle churning of the paddlewheel and the sound of the steam whistle added to the old-world charm.

As we stood on the open deck, the breeze carried laughter and music from nearby lands, making this peaceful cruise a delightful contrast to the excitement of the park; a serene voyage through Disney's timeless storytelling. During the ride, the steamboat made a gentle loop around Tom Sawyer Island, offering lovely views of Frontierland, Liberty Square, and the Haunted Mansion, along with stretches of natural scenery and charming period-style river scenes.

We soon cheered up with the *Pirates of the Caribbean* boat ride: dark, mysterious, and full of lively pirate scenes inspired by the movie. Afterwards, we tried on pirate hats at the nearby souvenir shop, laughing at how we looked in them.

Next, we boarded the train again and returned to the main area, where we enjoyed the charming *Tiki Room Show*; a lively performance featuring singing tropical birds and dancing flowers. Finally, we ended our park visit with the *Jungle Cruise*, a fun-filled boat journey through tropical forests, waterfalls, and animatronic wild animals. Our witty lady guide kept everyone laughing with her hilarious commentary, making it a truly delightful finale to a magical day.

By the time we finished, it was nearly 5:30 p.m. Just then, my dear friend Dr. Tyagaraj called to say he had arrived. He had driven all the way from *Tampa* on Florida's Gulf Coast: about two and a half hours away, along with his wife, son, and daughter, just to meet us in Orlando.

He and I had been batchmates at the Veterinary College in Bangalore nearly forty years ago, and we had planned this reunion well in advance. Seeing him again after so many years was truly heartwarming; a moment filled with nostalgia and joy. We met near the entrance of the park, and the years seemed to melt away in an instant. Warm handshakes quickly turned into heartfelt hugs as we caught up on old memories and shared stories from our college days.

Later, during the drive back to our hotel in his car, he introduced his family. They were equally delightful, and together we spent time chatting, laughing, and reminiscing about those carefree student years in Bangalore. Over a couple of pegs of Scotch and some snacks, our conversation flowed as effortlessly as it had in our college days, each story unearthing memories we had tucked away for decades.

His family was meeting us for the first time, yet there was an instant warmth; as if we had known them for years. Their smiles, their shared joy, and the way they joined our conversations made the reunion feel complete. Later, we drove to *Bawarchi Biryanis, Orlando*, for Andhra-style biryani, where the comforting aroma of spices filled the air. Over plates of fragrant chicken biryani and fiery starters, our conversations grew livelier and our hearts lighter.

It was one of those evenings that stay with you long after they end: an unforgettable blend of friendship, nostalgia, and the simple joy of being reunited after a lifetime. It was close to midnight when they dropped us back at the hotel. Though it was late and he still had a long 2.5-hour drive home, he seemed content; his children took turns driving back. We bid them a heartfelt goodbye and went to our room, happy and grateful.

A magical day, made even more special by the joy of rediscovering an old friendship.

Day 3: Wonders of the Deep at SeaWorld, Orlando

A Splash of Fun and Adventure

We left by bus at 8:30 a.m. after breakfast to spend a full day at *SeaWorld Orlando*. Our tour manager purchased our entry tickets and informed us that the bus would return to the same spot at 6:30 p.m. to pick us up. SeaWorld, we soon discovered, is a completely cashless park; everything must be paid for by card.

Our first stop was the *Dolphin Show*, held in a massive amphitheatre buzzing with excited visitors. The performance was simply fantastic: the dolphins leapt gracefully in perfect sync with their trainers, sending glistening arcs of water into the air and drawing delighted cheers from the crowd.

Next, we quite literally ran across the park, crossing a long wooden bridge to reach the *Orca Encounter*. The sight that greeted us was nothing short of majestic. The huge black-and-white killer whales glided through the water with effortless power, their sheer size both awe-inspiring and humbling. Yet, despite their power, they carried out each routine with remarkable precision, following their trainers' cues and receiving small fish treats after every successful feat.

The enormous stadium echoed with laughter and squeals as the whales sent giant waves crashing over the audience; water reaching all the way up to the fifteenth row. Thankfully, we had anticipated this and chosen seats in the eighteenth row. It was a breathtaking experience, one that left us marvelling at the beauty and grandeur of these magnificent creatures.

After the thrilling show, we headed straight to *Infinity Falls*, a circular raft ride designed for eight adventurers. The raft floated along an emerald-green artificial river, twisting past rocky landscapes before rising dramatically on a vertical elevator and plunging down a steep water chute. Neha had sensibly advised us to bring raincoats, but in our enthusiasm, we forgot; and the ride rewarded us with a spectacular soaking head to toe.

Luckily, the afternoon sun was bright and warm. We found a quiet spot nearby, letting the golden heat dry our dripping clothes. The paid dryers were both occupied by a family of six huddled inside like penguins, so we simply enjoyed the sunshine, the laughter, and the carefree pause before our next attraction. Soon, the *SeaWorld Parade* began, and Sunitha's eyes lit up with pure joy. After missing the Magic Kingdom parade the day before, she was finally living the moment she had been waiting for.

The parade was a dazzling spectacle, with floats and dancers adorned in shades of sea blue: some so pale they almost looked white, creating a mesmerizing oceanic theme. Cheerful SeaWorld mascots danced alongside, waving and moving in perfect rhythm to lively, infectious music. The energy was contagious, and we couldn't help but smile, cheer, and clap along with the crowd, swept up in the beauty and excitement of the show.

Next came the *Hydro Surge Show*, a breathtaking display of acrobatics and dance set to pulsating music. Every flip, jump, and synchronized splash left us spellbound, the performers moving with grace and precision that made the show feel magical.

Then followed the *Sea Lion Show*: hilarious, charming, and full of clever antics. The sea lions responded perfectly to their trainers' cues, swimming, diving, clapping their flippers, and winning the audience's hearts with their playful, mischievous personalities. Later, we attended *Rescue Tales*, a thoughtful presentation highlighting SeaWorld's dedication to rescuing and rehabilitating marine animals. While it lacked the spectacle of the earlier shows, it left a lasting impression, reminding us of the real-life heroes behind the scenes.

Finally, we visited the *Otters Exhibit*, where the lively, mischievous otters tumbled, slid, and splashed about, drawing laughter and delighted squeals from everyone around. Next, we entered the *Penguin Trek* area, peering through the glass to watch the penguins waddle, dive, and glide gracefully in their icy habitat. A few people inside, equipped with writing pads, appeared to be veterinarians or zoological staff, likely studying the penguins' behaviour; a fascinating glimpse into the work that goes on behind the scenes.

We skipped the roller coaster there, as bags and phones weren't allowed, and the automatic lockers seemed a bit tricky to operate, better safe than sorry. Afterward, we wandered into the *underwater aquarium tunnel*, walking through clear glass walls with glowing fish and graceful sharks swimming overhead. It was mesmerizing, as if we had stepped into another world beneath the waves. We even stopped to take pictures with performers on stilts and with two adorable *SeaWorld mascots:* a dolphin and a whale, creating fun memories to cherish from the day.

Throughout the day, we survived on a modest snack haul: a pack of cheese popcorn, three bottles of drinks (an energy drink, Coca-Cola, and Minute Maid orange juice), an energy bar, and a groundnut ladoo. Sunitha decided to skip lunch as nothing tempted her, not even the ice cream, which came in large double scoops.

Though we skipped the major thrill rides like *Journey to Atlantis, Pipeline Surf Coaster, Manta, and Mako*, just watching others on them: especially the Pipeline Surf Coaster, where riders stood upright, was enough to make our hearts race. By evening, we had thoroughly enjoyed the day: the perfect blend of marine magic, spectacular shows, and laughter made it truly unforgettable. It was a day of fun, wonder, and reflection; a SeaWorld experience that would linger in our memories for years to come.

We returned to the entrance by 6 p.m., where all our tour members had already gathered. The bus arrived promptly at 6:30 p.m., and we set off back to our hotel.

On the way, we stopped for dinner at *Aangan Grill and Bar*, where we enjoyed a hearty Indian meal after the long, exciting day. Before heading back, we did a bit of shopping nearby and picked up two Orlando-themed tote bags as souvenirs. Finally, we arrived at the hotel, took a short walk, then freshened up and packed for the next leg of our journey. Tomorrow, we would be checking out and driving to Miami.

SeaWorld had given us a day filled with splashes, surprises, and smiles, a perfect blend of adventure and wonder.

Day 17 - 18: The Road to Miami - Sunshine, Shopping, and the Sea

"From coast to coast, at the water's edge, the sun marks another chapter in our ever-unfolding journey."

Our Final Leg of the Tour

After breakfast at our hotel, the Crowne Plaza, Lake Buena Vista, Orlando, we packed our bags and checked out by 8:30 a.m., placing our luggage on the bus for the journey ahead. To our surprise, we learned that our long-time tour manager, Mr. Nalin Patel, who had been with us since the start of our trip, would be returning to New York, and that Ms. Nima from Chariot Travels would be taking over for the final leg of the tour. We bid a fond goodbye to Mr. Nalin, a soft-spoken and thorough gentleman, thanking him for his exceptional service and care throughout.

We began our road trip to *Miami*, our last destination, a five-hour drive through the sunny landscapes of Florida. En route, we stopped for lunch at *Palace Indian Restaurant*, where the meal was delicious and satisfying.

Later, the group made a stop at *Walmart*, as several members wanted to do some last-minute shopping. Having already visited Walmart twice in New Jersey with Neha and Abhishek, Sunitha and I simply wandered the aisles, helping a fellow traveller choose a MacBook laptop. We finally found him a great deal, a *MacBook for $700*, much cheaper than it would cost back in India.

Back on the bus, we requested our new tour manager to take us to see Miami Beach that very evening instead of resting, as many group members, including Sunitha and me, would be departing the next day for cruises or other destinations within the United States. Ms. Nima kindly agreed after discussing it with the driver, and soon we were heading toward the sparkling coast.

The drive ended at the famous *Miami Beach*, where we spent nearly two hours soaking in its vibrant atmosphere. The long stretch of soft sand, the clear turquoise water, and the rows of stylish cafes and restaurants created the perfect Miami mood. Some members stayed back to enjoy the nightlife, while most of us, including Sunitha and me, returned to the bus after a leisurely stroll and quiet moments by the water, capturing a few memories in photographs.

We returned to the bus and drove along *Ocean Drive*, just beyond the beach, bustling with its Art Deco buildings glowing in pastel lights, a signature of old-world Miami charm. Nearby, Lincoln Road Mall offered chic boutiques and outdoor cafés, while South Pointe Park Pier provided breathtaking views of the skyline and cruise ships sailing out to sea. The whole area pulsed with life, a lively mix of music, sea breeze, and joy that made us instantly fall in love with the city.

We finally checked into our hotel, the *Holiday Inn Express*, rested for a bit, and then left for dinner at *Bawarchi Biryani Restaurant*. The spread was wonderful, a mix of flavourful biryanis, spicy starters, and rich desserts, the perfect finale to a long day. After dinner, we returned to the hotel. Sunitha and I went for a short evening walk to enjoy the warm Miami breeze before turning in for the night. It had been a pleasant and fulfilling day, a fitting start to the final chapter of our unforgettable American adventure.

The Everglades, Miami Sights, and the Journey Home

Wild Waters, Art Streets, and Fond Farewells

Breakfast was served by 7:30 a.m., and we reported to the bus by 8:30 a.m. for our final day of sightseeing in *Florida*. Our first destination was the famous *Everglades National Park*, a vast subtropical wetland teeming with wildlife.

We boarded a thrilling *Airboat* and sped across the swamp, the enormous fans roaring behind us as the wind whipped our faces and the water sprayed gently around the raft. Tall grasses brushed past like a green blur, and shallow waters reflected the golden sunlight.

Thanks to our boat captain, who doubled as an engaging guide, we spotted wild alligators sunning themselves on the banks, elegant birds gliding above, and the lush, untamed beauty of the Everglades unfolding in every direction. The mix of speed, sights, and sounds made it exhilarating; a perfect introduction to this unique and wild landscape.

After the ride, we were guided through a small A*lligator Sanctuary*, where the caretakers shared fascinating facts about these creatures. Some brave visitors even held a baby alligator for a quick photo, for a small fee, of course. The experience was both adventurous and educational.

Next, we stopped for lunch at *Namaste Miami*, an Indian restaurant that was a delightful surprise. The spread featured a variety of chaats, starters, and authentic Indian dishes; flavours we hadn't savoured since the start of our tour. Every bite was delicious and thoroughly satisfying, a comforting reminder of home.

After lunch, our group set out on a *Biscayne Bay cruise*, a two-hour journey guided by an engaging narrator who shared fascinating details about the waterfront homes we passed. The warm breeze ruffled our hair as the sun sparkled off the turquoise waters, and we marvelled at the dazzling mansions of famous film stars, musicians, and business tycoons.

Each estate had its own private dock, with sleek yachts anchored gracefully alongside. On the horizon, a massive Virgin Atlantic cruise liner gleamed majestically, adding a sense of grandeur to the sparkling bay. The combination of sun, sea, and stunning views made it a truly unforgettable experience.

Once back on land, we spent a short while at the lively *Bayfront area*, where some tour members indulged in last-minute shopping. Soon after, we continued with our *Miami city tour*, eager to explore more of the city's vibrant streets, colorful neighbourhoods, and iconic landmarks.

Our guided tour took us through the city's highlights as well as some hidden gems. While bus access to the celebrity home district was now restricted for privacy, our guide compensated with lively storytelling and scenic stops that kept everyone engaged.

One of the most striking stops was *Muriel Street*, an open-air gallery where every wall had been transformed by local and international artists; a riot of colour, creativity, and imagination that brought the streets to life.

The guide, who owned a cozy coffee shop nearby, introduced us to authentic *Cuban coffee.* Sunitha and I gladly bought a cup each and savored it piping hot. Afterwards, we strolled around for half an hour, admiring the vibrant street art that brightened the neighborhood.

Next, we visited *Little Havana*, the heart of Miami's Cuban culture, known for its colorful houses and the locals' love of *Roosters*, considered symbols of good luck. The famous 8th Street buzzed with Latin music, cigar shops, and cheerful people.

We also passed by Bayfront Park, the *Frost Science Institute*, and later returned to another peaceful stretch of Miami Beach, where we relaxed by the sea and captured our final vacation photos.

Our guide pointed out the legendary *I-95 Highway*, a 2,300-mile road stretching all the way from Miami to Canada, truly a marvel of connectivity. We stopped briefly to browse through some roadside shops and restaurants before taking our final group photos, forty-four travellers who had shared 18 memorable days together.

This marked the *last day of our East and West Coast tour.* Wrapped in warm, salty ocean air, Miami was all rhythm and colour; a finale that felt like a celebration. A few of our fellow travellers had already left soon after breakfast, heading off for cruises or flights to other cities of United States. Sunitha and I, too, were preparing for our return to New Jersey via New York, after spending half a day on the city tour.

The rest of the group would continue exploring Miami until evening, enjoy a final dinner together, and eventually depart from Miami International Airport to Bangalore on their midnight flight. Later, we bid farewell to everyone, returned to our room for final packing, and checked out of the Holiday Inn Express. We booked a Lyft cab to *Fort Lauderdale Airport*, Terminal 3, to catch our return flight to New York.

Our three-hour flight took off at 5 p.m., and by 8 p.m., we had landed at *LaGuardia Airport, New York*, quite a distance from Neha's home in New Jersey. Onboard, they served snack packs with chips and crackers; I enjoyed a Pepsi, while Sunitha sipped on lemon soda.

Neha met us directly at Baggage Carousel 9, and together we began the journey home. We took a free shuttle bus from the terminal, followed by a subway train ride of about 30 minutes, then transferred to the PATH train at the World Trade Centre station, finally arriving at Journal Square. From there, we booked a cab to Neha's house, reaching it by 10:30 p.m.

It felt wonderful to freshen up, enjoy a home-cooked dinner, and chat with Neha and Abhishek about our incredible journey. The trip had been unforgettable: filled with sights, shared moments, and stories, but nothing matched the comfort of being back home with family. That night, we slept deeply, our hearts full and content after 18 extraordinary days across the United States.

Eighteen days, two coasts, countless moments; a journey that will forever remain etched in our hearts.

Adventures and Reflections: The East-West Coast Expedition

"From sunrise to sunset, coast to coast, every step became a story we would carry forever."

Our 18-day journey across the United States was a dream come true, meticulously arranged by Chariot Travels, Bangalore, and filled with unforgettable sights, experiences, and moments that will remain etched in our hearts. As we reflected on each city's unique charm, we felt immense gratitude for the experiences, friendships, and memories this journey gifted us.

We touched the sky in New York, walked with history in Washington, savoured sweetness in Hershey, felt the mist of Niagara, chased dreams in Los Angeles, glowed beneath the lights of Las Vegas, and stood at the edge of eternity at the Grand Canyon. San Francisco charmed us with its breezy elegance, Orlando lifted our spirits with childlike joy, and Miami wrapped us in its warm coastal embrace.

From the Pacific to the Atlantic, from majestic canyons to shining coasts, this journey became far more than travel; it became a quiet transformation. We finally returned to New Jersey, completing the circle of our memorable expedition, carrying not just photographs but a renewed sense of wonder: for the vastness of the world, the kindness of people, and the joy of discovering life beyond the familiar.

Eighteen days, thousands of miles, and countless memories later, we stood once more on the shores of the Atlantic, feeling the same breeze that had greeted us on the first day: yet now with fuller hearts, lighter spirits, and deeper gratitude. This expedition across America was not merely a journey across states; it was a journey through time, emotion, and the profound realization that the world is endlessly beautiful, waiting to be seen with open eyes and open hearts.

And yet, even as our coast-to-coast journey came to a graceful close, our hearts were not ready to stop exploring. After a brief two-day pause to rest and relive our memories, a new adventure awaited us: this time beyond the Atlantic horizon.

Our next path would not be traced by highways or city streets, but by the gentle sway of the ocean. With renewed excitement, we prepared to board the magnificent MSC Meraviglia for a seven-day cruise to the Bahamas: a voyage promising calm seas, sunlit islands, and a different kind of wonder.

If the United States revealed the power and diversity of the land, the cruise was ready to unveil the poetry of the sea. Our journey was far from over; it was simply turning the page to its next serene chapter.

SAILING INTO SERENITY:

7-DAY VOYAGE TO THE BAHAMAS - ABOARD MSC MERAVIGLIA

CHAPTER 7

SAILING INTO SERENITY: A 7-DAY VOYAGE TO THE BAHAMAS ABOARD MSC MERAVIGLIA

"When the ocean calls, you don't just travel, you surrender to its rhythm."

After a brief two-day pause following our whirlwind 18-day East and West Coast journey, we found ourselves yearning for one more adventure: a *seven-day cruise* from New York to the *Bahamas.* The morning dawned soft and grey, a gentle drizzle falling over New Jersey as our excitement quietly grew. It was finally the day our long-awaited voyage aboard MSC *Meraviglia* would begin: seven days of ocean breeze, sunshine, and serenity.

All three of us, Neha, Sunitha, and I, were ready by early morning. After a light snack, we packed our final essentials and rolled out our luggage: one 23-kg suitcase each, along with my backpack and Neha's and Suni's ever-trusty purses. Abhishek couldn't join us on this cruise due to his busy work schedule, but since it was the weekend, he kindly accompanied us to New York. Both Neha and Abhishek had cruised in the U.S. before, so their experience was invaluable, and it felt like a blessing to have our daughter with us to guide us through every step.

Umbrellas in hand, we walked to the nearby bus stop and boarded Bus No. 6 to Journal Square Station. From there, we caught the train to the World Trade Center Station, where the drizzle had softened into a fine mist, glistening against the towering glass buildings. We then transferred to a city bus headed toward *Clinton Wharf in Brooklyn*: the embarkation point at Terminal 10.

Day 1 - Boarding from New York: The Voyage Begins

By 10:30 a.m., we arrived at the port. The massive white MSC *Meraviglia* stood before us, gleaming under the cloudy sky; an architectural marvel resting gracefully along the *Hudson*. The moment felt surreal. Our luggage tags were already in place, so we joined the long queue to hand our bags to the cruise staff, who would send them directly to our *Cabin 9026 on Deck 9*. At the gate, we waved goodbye to Abhishek, who had come all the way to see us off. Then we entered the embarkation hall, where a sea of passengers stretched before us; thousands of excited voices blending into a lively hum. It took nearly an hour and a half to clear security and immigration, collect our *personalized MSC ID cards* (which also served as our room keys and onboard credit cards), and finally make our way across the gangway into the ship.

Stepping aboard the MSC *Meraviglia* felt like walking into a dream. The entrance deck shimmered with elegance: a grand *Swarovski crystal staircase* sparkling under soft, golden light, marble floors polished to perfection, and the faint scent of sea breeze mingling with perfume and fresh varnish. The cruise liner was nothing short of a *floating city*; with more than 5,000 guests and 1,200 crew members, every corner seemed alive with possibility. We first explored our cabin: a cozy, cleverly designed haven with a double bed, a single bed, soft ambient lighting, and a compact wardrobe that made efficient use of space. But it was the balcony that stole our hearts. The moment we stepped outside and saw the ocean stretching endlessly before us, it felt as though our adventure had truly begun.

Our luggage hadn't arrived yet, but we knew it would be delivered to our cabin before sail time, and the charm of the room made us forget all about it. Neha had already arranged for a bottle of *champagne*, a fruit bowl, and some starters to welcome us; thoughtful touches that instantly brought a smile to our faces.

We headed for lunch early, hoping to reach before the buffet area became too crowded. On Deck 15, the *Marketplace Buffet* unfolded before us: an endless spread of world cuisines, fresh salads, vibrant fruits, tempting desserts, and steaming coffee. It was overwhelming in the best possible way. I enjoyed a chilled Corona beer while we each chose our favourites. Every table offered a view of the ocean, and watching seagulls glide gracefully past as we dined felt like a simple yet perfect joy.

After lunch, we explored the ship, deck by deck, marvelling at its grandeur. Deck 5: called the *Colosseum*; featured a dazzling atrium that immediately caught our attention. From there, we made our way up through the higher decks, all the way to Deck 19, called the *Babylon*. Each level had its own unique charm. Even the deck names: *Taj Mahal, Grand Canyon, Acropolis, Tour Eiffel, Pyramids*; reflected the ship's global spirit and sense of wonder.

At 4 p.m., the *loud horn sounded*; the moment of departure. Everyone rushed to Deck 16, the open deck, to witness the most thrilling sight of all: the colossal MSC *Meraviglia* slowly gliding away from the harbour and making her way toward the *Verrazzano-Narrows Bridge*.

The clearance between the ship and the bridge was barely fourteen feet. As we watched the towering steel span pass just overhead, it was heart-stopping and magical all at once. Cameras clicked, cheers erupted, and for a moment it felt as though the entire ship held its breath in awe.

As we sailed further out, the Statue of Liberty gleamed in the distance, the Staten Island Ferry crossed our path, and the New York skyline melted into a soft silver haze. A pilot speedboat rode beside us briefly, guiding the massive vessel before peeling away; a cinematic touch to our real-life adventure.

Soon after, an announcement instructed all passengers to participate in the *mandatory safety drill.* We left our cabin and followed the staff's directions down to Deck 4, Zone A (Green), where our cards were scanned to confirm attendance. The elevators were closed for the drill, so we climbed the stairs back up to Deck 9; slightly winded but amused, and rested for a short while before dressing up for our first evening at sea.

As twilight fell, the ship came alive with music and colour. Photographers lined the promenade, capturing family portraits against the soft golden glow of the evening lights. We then made our way to our elegant fine-dining restaurant, *L'Olivo D'Oro*, on Deck 6, where a warm welcome awaited us from the ever-helpful hostess, the smiling manager, and the cheerful head waiter.

Our table, No. 816, was reserved exclusively for us for all seven nights, and we were looked after by a wonderful waitress and waiter whose warm smiles made every meal feel even more special. Dinner was exquisite. A basket of warm rolls and crisp breadsticks arrived first, setting the tone for the evening.

I began with a comforting onion broth soup, followed by a perfectly cooked steak served with mashed potatoes and beans, and raised a Heineken beer to toast the beginning of our voyage. Neha and Sunitha ordered their own favourites, each dish arriving beautifully plated. For dessert, we chose three different varieties so we could sample every flavour; and every bite felt celebratory.

After dinner, we strolled through the *Promenade* on Deck 5, where the ceiling burst into a breathtaking digital light show, a galaxy of stars and dancing colours glistening above us. We peeked into the casino, paused to enjoy a talented solo drummer performing on Deck 6, and then booked our seats for the Rock

Circus Show at the Carousel Lounge for a later date, since the limited seating operated on a first-come, first-served basis.

The night ended with a lively *Glow Party*, where guests danced under neon lights as a live band filled the air with upbeat tunes. Laughter, music, and the cool sea breeze created an atmosphere impossible to resist. Around midnight, pleasantly tired yet exhilarated, we returned to our cabin, enjoyed the starters Neha had arranged earlier, and stepped onto the balcony for one last look at the dark, glimmering Atlantic. *It had been a perfect first day, filled with joy, wonder, and the gentle excitement of knowing the sea would cradle us for the next seven days.*

Day 2 - At Sea: Life Aboard the Floating City

The day began early, with the sun softly filtering through our balcony curtains and the gentle rhythm of the ship gliding over the *Atlantic*. Neha was already up and gone; she had left for her Zumba and aerobics classes on Deck 15. Half an hour later, I joined her, camera in hand, capturing her energetic moves with the sea as her backdrop. The deck was alive with music and laughter, passengers of all ages following the lively instructor, their silhouettes outlined against the endless blue horizon.

After the class, Sunitha joined us, and together we made our way to the Marketplace Buffet for breakfast. The spread was once again lavish: freshly baked croissants, pancakes, tropical fruits, eggs made to order, and rich coffee. With the open ocean stretching endlessly beyond the glass windows, every meal felt like a feast for the senses. Once breakfast was done, we headed to the ship's main theatre, where the cruise director, Christopher

Caress, hosted an informative slideshow outlining the entire seven-day itinerary.

The session gave us a wonderful overview:

Day 1: Departure from *New York*
Day 2: At *Sea*
Day 3: *Port Canaveral* (1 p.m. to 9 p.m.); Shore excursion booked.
Day 4: *Nassau, Bahamas* (1 p.m. to 9 p.m.); Shore excursion booked.
Day 5: *Ocean Cay* (9 a.m. to 10 p.m.); MSC's private island for snorkelling, swimming,
a lighthouse trek, and an evening dance party.
Days 6 and 7: At *Sea*: Cruise activities, gala dinner, white and floral theme parties, photo session with the captain, and more.

As the plans unfolded on the big screen, we could feel our excitement building; every destination promised something new and unforgettable.

By noon, we decided to try a different fine-dining restaurant, *Panorama,* on Deck 6, for lunch. The elegant setting, attentive service, and gourmet dishes made it a wonderful experience, a perfect balance between luxury and leisure. Afterward, we took a leisurely stroll along Deck 7, pausing outside to admire the bright *orange lifeboats* and the vast expanse of sea beyond them. The ocean stretched endlessly into the horizon, a deep, hypnotic blue shimmering under the noon sun.

Neha then suggested we ride the *glass elevator* she had discovered earlier. It turned out to be a fantastic idea. As we ascended through the decks, a sweeping panoramic view of the ship's exterior unfolded before us, with endless ocean vistas stretching out in every direction. It truly felt like being suspended between sky and sea. Later in the afternoon, we picked up our shore excursion tickets for the next day's *Space Coast Highlights* tour, scheduled to begin at 3 p.m. after we docked.

Back in our cabin, we changed into swimwear and made our way to Deck 16. The warm afternoon sun, the bubbling *Jacuzzi*, and the cool splash of the pool made for a perfect combination of relaxation and fun. We lounged there for a while, watching the waves shining like silver ribbons against the moving ship.

At 1:45 p.m., we found seats in the theatre once again; this time for a live *Hypnosis Show* by none other than our cruise manager, Christopher Caress, who surprised us by revealing that he was also a professional hypnotist. What followed was pure magic. His performance was captivating, with volunteers on stage slipping effortlessly under his spell, gasps of surprise and astonishment filling the hall. We watched, completely fascinated, barely blinking. At the end of the show, he announced a special follow-up session on hypnosis as therapy, which we instantly booked for a later date.

By early evening, we were back in our room, freshened up and ready for the much-awaited *Gala Night*. Neha opened the pre-ordered bottle of champagne, and we toasted to our voyage and the beautiful moments already unfolding.

Dressed in our formal attire: a suit for me and cocktail dresses for Neha and Sunitha, we headed down for photographs. The ship's photographers captured several stunning portraits of the four of us with the ship's Captain and beside the Swarovski crystal staircase, perfectly highlighting the warm glow of the evening.

Dinner at L'Olivo D'Oro was a grand affair. The staff welcomed us warmly, and the meal was exquisite; from starters to dessert, every dish felt like a work of art. Afterwards, we strolled along the promenade, where the ceiling light show transformed the deck into a shifting spectacle of gold, violet, and sapphire.

At 9:15 p.m., we attended a spectacular *musical theatre show*, a performance that took us through the world of MSC cruises with dazzling choreography, opera, and vibrant costumes by a French troupe. The dancers and singers were extraordinary, a world-class production that left us applauding till the very end.

But the night wasn't over yet. By 10:15 p.m., the *Silent Disco Party* had taken over the promenade. Each of us received a headset after scanning our cabin card. Three channels: green, orange, and red, offered different genres of music; allowing everyone to dance to their own rhythm beneath the starlit sky. It was both surreal and hilarious to watch people moving to completely different beats at the same time. With Neha's help, we kept switching between channels, losing ourselves in the rhythm and the carefree energy. The atmosphere was electric, pure joy and freedom beneath the ship's glowing ceiling.

By 11:30 p.m., exhilarated yet tired, we paused for a few more pictures near the gleaming Swarovski staircase before returning to our cabin. Outside, the sea lay calm and moonlit, and the faint hum of the ship drifted through the night; steady, soft, and soothing. After a quick shower, we slipped into bed, still smiling, the laughter and music from the night lingering softly in our minds as we drifted to sleep.

Day 3 - Port Canaveral: The Space Coast Adventure

The morning began with the gentle sway of the ship and sunlight streaming softly through the curtains. We freshened up quickly and headed for breakfast, where a lavish spread awaited us: fresh fruits, warm baked breads, made-to-order eggs, and aromatic coffee. The day promised excitement: it was our first port of call, *Port Canaveral*, the gateway to Florida's Space Coast.

After breakfast, we strolled to the *Galleria Promenade*, where a lively preview show called the *Carousel Street Performance* was about to begin. It served as a teaser for the Rock Circus Group, a high-energy act that required a separate booking. Their acrobatic feats, vibrant costumes, and dazzling choreography were captivating enough to convince us, even though we had already reserved tickets for the full show on a later day.

From there, we climbed up to Deck 16, where a dance class was in full swing. Neha joined the energetic group, following the rhythm of the instructor's moves, while we strolled around, enjoying the open-air decks and the endless ocean views. Soon, a faint outline of land appeared on the horizon; *Florida's coastline coming into view.*

The ship was scheduled to dock in about ninety minutes. We took several photographs of the approaching port, marvelling at the massive vessel as it gracefully manoeuvred through the waters.

By around 1:30 p.m., the MSC *Meraviglia* docked smoothly at Port Canaveral.

We collected our passports, cabin cards, water and snacks before heading to the exit. The staff scanned our cards and verified our identities before allowing us to step ashore. Outside, the Florida sun greeted us warmly, its brightness tempered by a gentle ocean breeze.

Neha decided to stay back near the ship to swim and enjoy some water sports, while we joined our shore excursion group for the *"Space Coast Highlights"* tour. A comfortable, air-conditioned bus awaited us, and soon we were driving through the scenic streets of Cape Canaveral, ready for the day's adventure.

Our local guide was lively and exceptionally well-informed. He narrated fascinating stories about America's space history, pointing out landmarks as we passed them. He even handed out old newspaper clippings and photos of past space missions, making the history feel tangible and real.

Our first stop was the *U.S. Space Walk of Fame Museum and Space View Park*, dedicated to the astronauts of the Project Gemini and Apollo missions. The area was lined with granite slabs and sculptures commemorating the missions, each name etched in stone. Walking there felt like stepping through decades of human ambition and courage.

From the park, we made our way to a nearby bridge that offered a distant but clear view of the *Kennedy Space Center*. Its gigantic hangars and rocket launch pads rose through the morning haze. Our guide pointed out each area, explaining how launches were meticulously prepared and controlled, making the engineering marvels come alive before our eyes.

Nearby, memorials stood solemnly, honouring lost missions and heroes: the *SS Leopoldville,* sunk during World War II, and plaques remembering the sacrifices of *Desert Storm* and the *Gulf War.* We paused at the *Project Mercury* monument, where the handprints of pioneering astronauts were preserved, and then admired the brass sculpture depicting the Apollo program with a bust of President John F. Kennedy (1961) watching over it.

I felt a lump in my throat when we reached the plaques for the *Challenger and Columbia crews,* especially seeing *Kalpana Chawla's* name, one of India's most beloved astronauts. The courage and sacrifice of these space travellers echoed deeply in that quiet park.

We learned that *a Rocket Launch was scheduled for the next morning at 4 a.m.,* and the thought of standing so close to history in the making sent a thrill through all of us. As we continued, our guide pointed excitedly to the horizon, and there it was: a rocket standing tall on the launchpad, poised for liftoff the next day. I zoomed in with my camera and managed to capture a close shot from a nearby beach, committing the powerful sight to memory.

Coincidentally, one of the four crew members and the *mission's Pilot was an Indian, Subhanshu Shukla.* It felt special to witness a moment of shared pride.

While returning to the bus, I noticed two huge *Turkey Buzzards* perched on a wooden signpost, like dark sentinels overlooking the coast. Their wings stretched wide against the sky; a striking image of nature standing tall amid human progress.

By 6:45 p.m., we were back at the port. The setting sun bathed the MSC Meraviglia in golden light; she looked magnificent from the outside. We took a few photos before calling Neha, who was waiting for us just past the security checkpoint. After re-scanning our cards, we boarded and made our way back to our cabin.

A quick shower and change later, we were ready for dinner. The fine dining restaurant once again exceeded expectations; elegant, flavourful, and perfectly served. Afterwards, at 9 p.m., we attended a Broadway-style live performance themed around country and western music. Soulful songs, cowboy hats, and foot-tapping rhythms filled the theatre, transporting us straight into the heart of Americana.

When the show ended, we made our way to the Promenade Dome, where the night's main event, the *"Space Party,"* was already in full swing. The same talented dancers and singers from the previous night now appeared in glowing, neon-lit space costumes, performing beneath a dazzling digital dome that projected images of astronauts, galaxies, and swirling constellations. The atmosphere was electric; a pure cosmic celebration.

We even managed to capture some wonderful photos of Neha with the performers before calling it a night. By the time we returned to our cabin, it was midnight. Tired, happy, and awestruck, we reflected on a day that had truly taken us from the earth to the stars.

Day 4 - Nassau, The Bahamas: Sun, Sea, and the White Party

We woke up a little later than usual, the gentle hum of the ship and the endless blue of the sea beyond our balcony setting the perfect lazy-morning mood. After freshening up, we made our way to the buffet for a delicious breakfast: platters of fresh fruits, pancakes, eggs, croissants, and steaming, aromatic coffee. The plan for the day was simple: explore more of the ship and, later, step ashore at *Nassau*, the vibrant capital of the *Bahamas*.

After breakfast, we decided to check out some areas we had missed earlier, including the sports deck, gym, children's zone, motocross track, and the gaming area on Deck 17. It was fascinating to see the range of activities available, from bowling alleys to a virtual reality room. Neha was especially excited to try the flight simulator before the trip ended, her enthusiasm infectious as we wandered through the lively spaces.

Soon, we made our way to Deck 16, eager to watch as the ship approached Nassau's shores. The sight that unfolded was breathtaking: turquoise waters, a palm-fringed coastline, and the majestic Atlantis Resort, rising like a coral-pink castle on Paradise Island. It brought to mind the famous Atlantis Hotel in Dubai, equally grand and enchanting.

As we neared the port, three other massive cruise ships were already docked: *Royal Caribbean's Radiance of the Seas, Carnival Glory,* and the elegant *Disney Dream*, their decks alive with excited travellers.

Our ship, the *MSC Meraviglia*, was the largest of them all. Together, the fleet looked like a floating city of dreams. We were told that sometimes as many as eight cruise ships could dock in Nassau at once; what a spectacular sight that must be.

We enjoyed an early lunch at the Marketplace Buffet, relishing the wide variety of cuisines before setting out for our afternoon excursion. By 1 p.m., the three of us, Neha, Sunitha, and I, passed through security, had our cruise cards scanned, and disembarked. Neha, who had visited Nassau on a previous trip, chose to stay near the harbour, exploring the colourful local markets before returning to the ship for some relaxed pool time.

Meanwhile, Sunitha and I set off on our *Bay Area Catamaran and City Tour*, a pre-booked half-day adventure complete with unlimited drinks and light snacks, promising a perfect mix of sightseeing and leisure on the sparkling Bahamian waters.

Our Group 8 was one of eleven or twelve groups that had booked onboard separate catamarans for the tour, each comprising around twenty passengers. Soon, we were led to the ferry terminal, where our sleek catamaran, *"Seahorse,"* awaited. The vessel was cheerful and lively, with upbeat music playing and a friendly crew circulating with trays of *Bahama Mama* and *Bahama Papa*, the island's signature rum cocktails. The cruise began in a haze of laughter and sunshine, the salty Caribbean breeze blending perfectly with the rhythm of the music.

As we sailed past the harbour, we passed the giant cruise liners, each magnificent in design, and waved at the guests on deck. Our guide, an energetic and witty Bahamian, kept us entertained with his continuous commentary, sharing stories and local titbits with infectious enthusiasm. In the distance, the

Atlantis Resort gleamed, its towers rising above the turquoise waters. Private islands owned by celebrities dotted the horizon, and luxury yachts bobbed gently near oceanfront mansions, a glimpse into a world of leisure and opulence.

Our guide pointed out homes belonging to film stars, singers, and sports legends, and even mentioned a small nearby island where tourists could take boat trips to feed and play with tiny pigs, the famous *"Pig Beach."* We all laughed at the thought of it.

The scenery was postcard-perfect: aquamarine waters, white sandy beaches, and palm-dotted islands stretching as far as the eye could see. Along the way, we even spotted an *old pirate ship*, now used for themed boat rides, looking as though it had sailed straight out of a movie. Drinks and snacks flowed freely. I sampled a couple of Bahama Papas, a can of Bahamian beer, and some chips.

We met a lovely family of four from Pennsylvania; a friendly couple traveling with their son and daughter, who, like us, were fellow passengers from the cruise ship. We spent a delightful hour together, chatting, laughing, and soaking up the golden sunshine. It felt as though we had known them for ages.

After about an hour, the catamaran glided back to a small dock, where we bid farewell to the cheerful crew; the two smiling attendants who had served us so graciously, our animated guide, and the captain. I left a small tip of $10 in appreciation before we boarded our tour bus for the next leg of the day.

The *city tour of Nassau* took us through charming lanes lined with pastel-coloured colonial buildings, bustling markets, and streets filled with locals radiating the island's relaxed spirit. We visited *Fort Fincastle,* the *Straw Market,* the *Marina*, and again caught a close-up view of the majestic *Atlantis Resort*, its coral-pink towers rising gracefully above the city.

The bus made a brief stop for shopping, and we made the most of it. We picked up bags, purses, a Nassau hat, Bahamas T-shirts, four shot glasses, and some magnets as keepsakes. We had planned to get the famous *Bahamas Rum Cakes*, but Neha had already promised to buy them during her stroll near the shore, selecting three delicious flavours for us to take back to Bangalore.

The tour ended around 5 p.m., and the bus brought us back to the ship, where we went through the usual security checks before stepping aboard again. Tired but exhilarated, we stopped by the buffet for coffee and light snacks, and Neha soon joined us.

Later, we returned to our cabin to freshen up and change into party wear. Tonight was the much-anticipated *White Party* on Deck 15, one of the ship's grandest events. We all dressed in white, joining thousands of guests who shared the same elegant theme.

Before the festivities began, we enjoyed our fine-dining dinner at L'Olivo D'Oro, where the atmosphere was festive, and the staff greeted us with song and dance, creating a joyful start to the evening. The food, as always, was exquisite.

After dinner, we made our way up to Deck 15, where the poolside stage came alive with music and lights. Guests in shimmering white swayed, sang, and danced under the open sky. Even the lively Cruise Director and crew joined in on stage, dancing alongside everyone and keeping the energy high.

From Deck 16, more guests cheered, watched, and joined in the fun. It was magical: music, laughter, sea breeze, and sparkling white lights blending into one unforgettable night.

By midnight, we finally returned to our cabin; tired, happy, and still humming the tunes of the evening. A quick shower, a few smiles exchanged, and we drifted off to sleep, hearts full of island magic.

Day 5 - Ocean Cay Island: A Day in Paradise

Today, we woke up early, as we were scheduled to reach port by 9 a.m. for a full day at MSC Cruises exclusive island, Ocean Cay. After an early breakfast, we packed our backpacks with swimming gear, spare clothes, and snorkelling equipment, and headed out of the ship by 9 a.m. We were set to spend the entire day on Ocean Cay (9 a.m. to 9 p.m.). What a fabulous time it turned out to be.

Ocean Cay Highlights:

Ocean Cay, MSC's private island in the Bahamas, felt like a slice of paradise crafted for pure relaxation. Surrounded by crystal-clear waters and stretches of soft white sand, the island offered multiple beaches, tranquil lagoons, and coral coves perfect for snorkelling or kayaking.

Its 100-foot lighthouse, which transforms into a beacon of lights after sunset, stood as the island's most iconic landmark. With tropical cocktails in bars, beachside grills sizzling, hammocks swaying under palm trees, and music drifting into the night, Ocean Cay felt less like a stop on the cruise and more like a dream brought to life.

We left the ship and made our way to the pre-booked *Lighthouse tour,* eager for the view from the top. Our guide warned us that the climb was strenuous and had to be done level by level, advising anyone who felt discomfort not to continue, as he would need to escort them back down. One family with a small child had to stop after the first level when the little girl felt dizzy, and the guide kindly accompanied them while we waited.

As we resumed our ascent, he continued explaining the history and features of the lighthouse. The climb was indeed tough. But when we reached the third level, about ten floors up, we were rewarded with a breathtaking panorama. The entire island lay stretched out below us, and our magnificent cruise ship glistened in the turquoise waters like a jewel.

Wandering across the island afterward, I paused to sip a refreshing Corona beer, soaking in the warm sun and gentle sea breeze. The island itself was stunning, with its landscape dotted by seven or eight beaches, each worth a visit.

The first beach Neha took us to had a lovely rocky stretch on one side, perfect for *snorkelling*. She ventured boldly into the deeper waters while we stayed closer to the shore, and the experience was nothing short of amazing. Slipping into the crystal-clear, shallow waters, we snorkelled among schools of small white fish and medium-sized yellow ones. Suddenly, a graceful *manta ray* glided past us, disappearing as quickly as it had appeared. Neha skillfully captured every moment with her underwater camera, preserving the magic of the day.

Lunch was served at one of the open-air shacks: burgers, French fries, mac 'n' cheese, and chilled Coke, simple yet delicious. After that, we walked across the entire island. It was hot and sunny, and by the end of it we were thoroughly tanned, with our clothes and shoes full of sand. Our next stop was a second beach, lined with beach chairs and buzzing with children and families enjoying themselves. We took plenty of photos there. To our surprise, the ship's photographer even showed up to take pictures of guests with their families, and we had a couple of fun shots taken in the water.

In the afternoon, we visited yet another beach to swim and unwind. Before leaving, we posed for photos seated in a small, decorated *wooden boat with the title Ocean Cay* and the MSC emblem; perfect keepsakes. After drying off, I treated myself to a tropical delight: a *Pina Colada cocktail* (rum, cream of coconut, and pineapple juice), served in a pineapple-shaped container, which I kept as a cheerful souvenir.

After soaking in the sun and sea, we returned to the ship for a refreshing bath and dinner. Soon after, we headed back to the beach for the *Beach and Lighthouse Party*, which began with a dazzling light display from the towering lighthouse, accompanied by music that filled the night air.

The live band's energy was infectious, and they were joined by the troupe from the ship, who encouraged everyone to join in and follow their dance steps. It was great fun. Neha, a lovely dancer, matched them step for step. While Sunitha and I joined in for a short while before settling back to enjoy the lively atmosphere as the dancing continued late into the night.

By 8:30 p.m., we were back on board. The cruise ship departed sharply at 9 p.m., and by then we were already immersed in the *Country-Western* music show, followed by the electrifying *Tropical Party* on Deck 15, a carnival of lights, colour, and rhythm that carried on well past midnight. At last, we called it a night and returned to our cabin, hearts full and spirits high.

Day 6 - Indulgence and Entertainment at Sea

We woke up late and decided to take it easy, letting the rhythm of the ship guide our day. After freshening up, Neha suggested we skip our routine breakfast and try something different.

Our morning began with a sweet treat at *Jean Philippe Chocolat and Cafe*, where we savoured their rich hot chocolate topped with ice cream: pure bliss and surprisingly filling too. We followed it up with freshly made crepes, delicate and delicious, at the *Jean Philippe Crepe and Gelato* shop nearby. A wonderful change of taste, thanks to Neha.

The morning drifted by gently as we wandered through the Promenade, taking in its lively bustle. The soft hum of music, the aroma of fresh chocolate, and the glittering boutique displays created a bright, festive atmosphere. Families clicked photos, couples browsed the shops, and children darted around excitedly, adding to the ship's cheerful energy.

Soon, we made our way to the *Live Chocolate-making demonstration*. It was fascinating to watch the main chocolatier at work. With confident, practiced movements, he poured silky molten chocolate into a detailed mould to create an exact miniature replica of the MSC Meraviglia.

As the mould set, he explained the process, sharing little tips and fun facts about chocolate craftsmanship. The warm, rich aroma of cocoa filled the room, and the best part came at the end: tasting freshly prepared samples that were smooth, warm, and utterly delicious.

By lunchtime, we headed to the restaurant opposite our fine dining area. It was bright and buzzing with activity, the rhythm of clinking cutlery blending with cheerful conversations. We enjoyed another hearty meal before stepping out for a relaxed walk around the decks. The gentle sea breeze brushed past us as the vast blue ocean glimmered in the afternoon sun, offering the perfect, peaceful end to our leisurely morning.

In the afternoon, we settled into the theatre for a thrilling show titled *"Faith in Hypnosis,"* presented by our cruise director and hypnotist, Mr. Chris. The excitement in the room was palpable. Before beginning, he firmly announced that he needed *pin-drop silence*, adding that families with young children might prefer to step out, as the session required deep concentration and complete quiet.

The room instantly grew still, the anticipation rising like a silent wave. Before the performance even began, he asked the entire audience to stand and follow a series of simple commands. It was astonishing to see how quickly and effortlessly some people responded, almost as if their minds were already tuned to his voice. *From that first round, he began picking volunteers straight from the crowd.* The selected group was then brought onstage, where he put them through another round of rapid, intense hypnosis; accepting some, rejecting others, until he finally narrowed it down to about *15 volunteers*, seated in chairs across the dais.

Once the final 15 volunteers were seated on the dais: the atmosphere in the theatre shifted from playful curiosity to deep anticipation. Mr. Chris walked slowly along the row of chairs, speaking to each person with calm assurance. He asked them why they wanted to be hypnotised; what they hoped to heal.

Their answers were heartfelt and varied: *fear of heights, fear of darkness, fear of spiders, a few wanting to break habits like smoking, one person struggling with a lack of confidence, and several others with personal worries* they wished to overcome. Each reason was different, each one deeply human. He then guided them back into a trance with astonishing ease. One moment they were responding to his questions, and the next, they slipped back into stillness, as if someone had dimmed a light inside them.

Moving from one volunteer to the next, he gave each person specific, personalised suggestions: gentle instructions tailored to their fear, habit, or emotional block. His voice was steady, soothing, and strangely compelling, filling the theatre with an almost sacred silence.

What followed was nothing short of mind-blowing. With just a snap of his fingers: these otherwise normal, *wide-awake people suddenly collapsed like lifeless rag dolls*, their bodies going limp instantly, as if someone had switched them off. The entire audience gasped in disbelief. Watching real people slip so smoothly into a trance right before our eyes felt like witnessing the human mind surrender to another person's control: mysterious, powerful, and mesmerizing all at once.

By the end of the session, he snapped his fingers, bringing them back to full awareness. What followed felt nothing short of miraculous. When he asked them again about their fears, there were no tense expressions or hesitation; only calm, confident smiles. One by one, they said they felt better… lighter… stronger… that they would overcome it. The audience murmured in awe. Whether it was the power of mindset, suggestion, or sheer belief, it was a remarkable transformation to witness.

Later, we wandered to the British Pub, where I savoured a glass of Guinness Stout amid its cozy wooden interiors. From there, we continued to another *musical show* featuring opera-style performances, elegant voices soaring across the stage, accompanied by graceful dancers.

As the day mellowed, we stepped onto the open deck to watch the sun melt into the horizon. The sky transformed into sweeping shades of gold, pink, and violet, the ocean shining beneath it, a breathtaking finale to an extraordinary afternoon at sea.

At 10 p.m., we attended the much-awaited *Rock Circus Show*, which we had pre-booked with cocktails. The performance was electrifying with acrobats, dancers, and musicians blending rock music with circus artistry in a stunning visual spectacle. The energy was contagious, and we loved every minute of it.

Finally, at 11 p.m., we returned to the Promenade for the ship's final dance party. The atmosphere was jubilant, passengers and crew dancing together one last time before the voyage's end. I even tried my luck at the *Lotto* for fun, $10 for a chance at the $350,000 prize. Though no one won the mega prize, several smaller prizes were claimed, making it exciting just to participate.

By midnight, we returned to our cabin, filled with joy and a touch of nostalgia as our beautiful cruise journey neared its end.

Day 7 - Dolphins, Music, and Farewell to the High Seas

We woke up late this morning, savouring our final day at sea and letting the gentle rhythm of the ship set the tone. As Neha and I stood on our cabin's open deck, cameras in hand, we were treated to an unforgettable sight: *a pod of Dolphins* gracefully swimming alongside our ship. They leapt and dipped through the waves as if performing a private farewell show just for us. It truly felt like a parting salute from the ocean itself.

After capturing the magical moment on video, we made our way to the *Bamboo Pool buffet* for breakfast. The sea breeze was cool and refreshing, the atmosphere relaxed, and everyone around seemed to be enjoying the unhurried charm of the last morning aboard. The gentle sparkle of sunlight on the water made the meal feel even more delightful.

Later, Neha decided to take on the *Himalayan Bridge Challenge*, the adventurous rope course suspended high above the deck. It looked daunting from below: narrow planks, swinging ropes, and dizzying heights, yet she was absolutely thrilled, safely strapped into her harness as we cheered her on from the deck. Watching her walk confidently across the course against the backdrop of the open sea was both nerve-wracking and impressive.

From there, Neha led Sunitha and me to the legendary *waterslides at the Polar Aquapark* on Deck 19; a bright, twisting maze of tubes, turns, speed, and sudden splashes. Before we could dive in, we signed a waiver and picked up our wristbands; a calm, almost formal ritual before the chaos that awaited us. Neha, of course, was already an expert; she had conquered all three slides on earlier days while we were away on shore excursions. Now, it was our turn to feel the rush.

There were three slides in total: two meant for single or double tubes, and the heart-pounding *Champagne Glass slide*, where you plunged down with nothing but gravity guiding you through a narrow, twisting passage. We chose the *double tube*, with Neha in front, followed by Sunitha and me going one after another. Each of us climbed the stairs alongside Neha, our excitement growing with every step. At the top, the lifeguard gave us a simple nod; our cue to go

Suddenly we were off: twisting, spinning, and hurtling through the winding tube. A burst of cool darkness gave way to flashes of bright light as we swirled faster and faster, until a final plunge shot us out into the pool with an enormous splash that drenched us instantly. Breathless and laughing uncontrollably, we clung to our tube, hearts racing, adrenaline buzzing through every nerve.

It had been more than a decade since we had felt such wild, carefree excitement. Neha urged us to go again, and this time, with the first-time jitters gone, we embraced the ride fully: screaming, laughing, and surrendering to every twist and turn. Even after we reached the bottom, our hearts continued to pound, the thrill lingering long after the water had settled.

Next, we explored the gaming zone, where Neha eagerly tried the *Flight Simulator*, a paid experience that recreated the thrill of flying. She was enclosed in a closed capsule, which tilted, swayed, and spun to mimic take-off, loops, and sudden drops. From outside, we could hear her excited squeals of joy and thrilling screams echoing from within, while a screen displayed the path the simulator was taking: twisting through virtual clouds, looping over cities, and diving toward the ground.

When she finally stepped out, her cheeks were flushed and her eyes sparkling with excitement, a radiant mix of adrenaline and joy. Watching her exhilaration made us almost wish we could try it ourselves.

By afternoon, we joined the *Crew Talent Show*, hosted by our ever-energetic Cruise Director: a true whirlwind of charm, humour, and boundless enthusiasm. His presence lit up the stage and the audience alike, drawing cheers, laughter, and applause from everyone around. The energy was infectious, and for a few hours, the ship seemed to pulse with pure fun and camaraderie.

As we entered the hall for the show, each guest was handed a token either pink or blue with a serial number: setting the stage for a *surprise lottery*. To my delight, the Cruise Director suddenly called me on stage to pick the winning ticket. Wearing a bright yellow T-shirt, I was singled out with a playful, *"Let's get the guy in the yellow T-shirt to pick the winning number."*

He asked my name and was intrigued to learn that I was a doctor by profession. Standing there under the spotlight, laughing and a little starstruck, I felt completely caught up in the moment. In the end, a lady in the back row with a pink ticket emerged as the lucky winner: but the thrill of being part of the surprise was unforgettable.

Afterwards, we strolled along Deck 7 to take a closer look at the lifeboats: massive, imposing, and even more impressive up close. We couldn't help but recall watching the crew lower them during the safety drill at Ocean Cay: their precision, coordination, and calm efficiency had been truly admirable.

Later, at the Promenade, we were captivated by a stunning visual display celebrating some of the world's most beautiful destinations. The vibrant images and sweeping scenes felt like a fitting tribute as our own voyage drew to a close, a gentle reminder of the wonders we had experienced on this unforgettable journey.

We then indulged in a little souvenir shopping at the ship's gift store before heading to our fine dining restaurant for a special *Italian Night Dinner*. The staff greeted us with dancing and music, waving napkins in the vibrant colours of the Italian flag: red, white, and green. The atmosphere was lively and heartwarming, and the meal, as always, was exquisite, every bite a delight.

Post-dinner, we caught the *Bartenders' Juggling Show* on Deck 5: an entertaining blend of flair, precision, and playful humour. From there, we moved on to the spectacular *"Live by Meraviglia" musical*, featuring the ship's talented troupe of singers and dancers. The performances were breathtaking, bursting with colour, rhythm, and energy that seemed to fill every corner of the theatre. Later, we joined the *ABBA tribute show* at the Promenade, a nostalgic sing-along that transported us back to the songs of our youth.

Just when we thought the evening was winding down, Neha suggested we peek into *Karaoke Night at the TV Studio and Bar* on Deck 7: a high-tech studio with a lively dance floor and an enthusiastic, cheering crowd. On a whim, we registered our names, and soon both of us were on stage, singing one after the other as our names were announced. The audience clapped, cheered, and joined in, and in that moment, it felt like pure joy. The experience quickly becamc one of the happiest memories of the entire cruise, a perfect finale to our last night at sea.

By the time we returned to our cabin, it was nearly 1 a.m. We were tired but exhilarated after a perfect finale to our week at sea. We packed our bags, double-checked everything, and decided to carry our luggage ourselves in the morning to avoid delays. As we turned in for the night, the gentle hum of the ocean outside lulled us to sleep. Tomorrow, we would dock back in New York, bringing to close an unforgettable journey, seven magical days aboard the MSC cruise to the Bahamas.

Day 8 - Homecoming: New York City and New Jersey beckon us

We woke up very early, around 5 a.m., on the final morning of our cruise, hearts full of a quiet mix of nostalgia and gratitude. Before sunrise, Neha and I decided to relive a few of our favourite spots on the ship. We wandered to the 19th and 15th decks, dipping our feet into the jacuzzi and watching the still waters of the pool shimmer softly in the gentle morning light. The calmness of the sea and the crisp, fresh air made it feel like the perfect moment to pause and soak it all in.

As we lingered, our conversation drifted to past adventures: the thrill of snorkelling, the schools of tiny fish, and, most memorably, the graceful manta ray that had glided past us, captured forever on Neha's underwater camera. These were memories that felt etched into our hearts.

By 6 a.m., Sunitha joined us, and the three of us made our way to the buffet on Deck 15 for one last breakfast at sea. The familiar aroma of freshly brewed coffee, warm pastries, and the soft clatter of plates made us linger a little longer, savouring the simple pleasure of the morning and the gentle rhythm of the ship before it carried us back to land.

Afterwards, we took a final stroll around the ship, wandering from the Promenade to the open decks, taking in every view as if trying to hold onto the magic just a little longer. The ship glided gently toward Brooklyn Harbor, bringing our unforgettable week at sea to a close. Once we had finished the last bits of packing, chargers, toiletries, and travel documents, we stepped out onto our cabin balcony one final time. The cool dawn breeze carried the fresh scent of the sea, and in the distance, the faint outline of the New York Bridge came into view.

Watching our massive ship glide gracefully beneath it was a moment of awe and reflection, a picture-perfect finale to our unforgettable journey at sea. Afterwards, we cleared our personal expense bills at the kiosks and prepared to disembark. The MSC Meraviglia finally docked at the same New York City port from which we had set sail exactly a week ago, marking the end of a voyage filled with laughter, adventure, and memories to last a lifetime.

The announcement came for our floor, and we rolled our luggage through the busy corridors to Deck 5, joining hundreds of fellow passengers as we bid farewell to the crew and the ship. Before leaving, I took a moment to thank the wonderful staff: from the housekeeping team, who kept our rooms spotless every day (even after the sandy aftermath of Ocean Cay), to the cheerful dining crew, who made every meal a delight. *The service gratuity of 120 USD per person for the seven days felt truly well-deserved and heartfelt.*

What amazed us most was learning that many of these staff members, including the captain and cruise director, work eight months straight without leaving the ship, welcoming new guests every week with the same energy, warmth, and smiles. Their dedication deserves nothing less than a salute.

Immigration was smooth and quick, and soon we were stepping back onto firm land. The cruise company generously provided free ferry tickets into the city, and as we boarded, we spotted Abhishek waiting to greet us with his ever-ready smile: a comforting, familiar sight after our ocean adventure. Together, we took the ferry to Wall Street, then the train from the World Trade Centre station to New Jersey.

Back home, Neha and Abhishek treated us to a delicious homemade lunch. We rested for a while, still carrying the gentle sway of the sea in our minds, as if the rhythm of the cruise lingered long after we had left the water behind. Later that evening, at 4 p.m. sharp, I went up to Neha and Abhishek's terrace to watch our majestic ship, the MSC Meraviglia, sail away once more from Brooklyn Port, embarking on her next voyage.

A week earlier, Abhishek had stood there watching her depart with us on board. Today, as I watched her glide into the horizon, I whispered a quiet thank you: for the sea, the sky, the memories, and God's grace that had kept us safe and joyful through it all. It had truly been an memorable seven-day cruise to the Bahamas. Filled with laughter, adventure, discovery, and gratitude, it was a perfect finale to an unforgettable journey at sea.

Reflections – The Sea Within

"The sea, once it casts its spell, holds one in its net of wonder forever."

– Jacques Cousteau

As our voyage aboard the MSC Meraviglia came to an end, what lingered was not just the memory of the destinations, *New York City, Port Canaveral, Nassau, and Ocean Cay*, but the feeling of being part of something vast and timeless.

Each day on the ship carried its own rhythm: mornings filled with laughter and exploration, evenings alive with music and celebration, and nights when the sea whispered secrets only travellers can hear.

From the Zumba sessions and gala dinners to the space coast adventures and white-sand beaches of the Bahamas, every moment felt painted in shades of joy and wonder. The turquoise waters of Nassau, the starlit Ocean Cay, and the deep blue calm of the open sea all became pages in our memory's diary.

But more than the sights and sounds, it was the feeling of togetherness that defined this cruise: shared laughter, spontaneous dances, late-night shows, and conversations that flowed as freely as the ocean breeze.

Watching dolphins at dawn, tasting pina coladas under the lighthouse, and singing karaoke on the final night were not just events, they were heartbeats of an unforgettable journey. Even in quiet moments alone on the deck, gazing at the endless horizon, there was a profound sense of perspective: how vast and unhurried the ocean is, and yet how intimate it feels when shared with loved ones.

The gentle rocking of the ship, the rhythm of the waves, and the golden glow of the sunset reminded us that life itself is a journey best savoured, not rushed. And in those hours of reflection, we realized that the true treasures of this voyage were not souvenirs or photos, but the simple, fleeting moments that made us laugh, pause, and feel fully alive.

Relationships rekindled, spontaneous joy, the shared awe at nature's beauty: these were the pearls we carried back with us, tucked into the corners of memory.

When the Meraviglia finally returned to New York, it seemed as though the sea had gifted us something deeper: a renewed sense of gratitude, calm, and connection. We came back with sand in our shoes, music in our minds, and the sea forever in our hearts. What had begun as a cruise ended as a pilgrimage of joy. For in those seven days, we discovered that serenity isn't found on distant shores, it is found within, when we allow ourselves to simply drift, breathe, and be.

It felt as though the ocean had prepared our hearts for what awaited us next: another journey, another set of memories waiting to unfold. And once home, we found ourselves looking forward with renewed excitement.

Neha and Abhishek had already planned our next adventure: a week-long holiday aligned with the Fourth of July celebrations.

This time, the road would lead us to Massachusetts, Boston, and the serene landscapes of Maine. We would reunite with friends and relatives, explore Acadia National Park, and savour the unique charm of America's Northeast.

After the magic of the Meraviglia, this new journey appeared like a continuation of the same thread of love, laughter, and exploration. With hearts still full from the sea and spirits lifted by anticipation, we stepped into the next chapter: ready to embrace new sights, reconnect with loved ones, and carry forward the quiet serenity the ocean had gifted us.

REUNION IN MASSACHUSETTS AND BOSTON

ARRIVAL IN MAINE FOR ACADIA NATIONAL PARK VISIT

CHAPTER 8

REUNION IN MASSACHUSETTS AND BOSTON-ARRIVAL IN MAINE FOR ACADIA NATIONAL PARK VISIT

"Reunions are not about going back; they are about rediscovering the warmth that never really left us."

This seven-day adventure unfolded beautifully, thanks to the meticulous planning of our daughter, Neha, and son-in-law, Abhishek. With the Fourth of July holiday week approaching, a perfect break in the U.S. calendar, they crafted an itinerary that blended family reunions, scenic drives, and unforgettable outdoor experiences.

Our journey began in Massachusetts, where I reconnected with my veterinary college classmates after decades. From there, we continued to Boston to meet our cousin and explore the iconic Freedom Trail, taking in the city's rich history and timeless charm.

After Boston, Neha and Abhishek planned a four-day getaway to Maine, booking a lovely Airbnb called Creekside Crib in Otis. This peaceful retreat became our base for an exciting schedule in and around Acadia National Park.

We planned to hike the stunning Ocean Path Trail, watch the magical 4 a.m. sunrise from Cadillac Mountain, wander through the Wild Gardens of Acadia, visit the scenic Bass Harbor Head Lighthouse, and stop at Hulls Cove Visitor Center before trekking around the serene Jordan Pond.

The itinerary also included exploring Bar Harbor and Bar Island, where the island dramatically disappears during high tide; walking along the Friends of the Shore Path to admire the remarkable Balance Rock; and visiting the tranquil Schoodic Peninsula.

On our return journey, we would stop at the historic Harvard University campus in Cambridge and enjoy a delightful meal at Saloniki Greek, rounding off a perfectly curated, memorable, and heartwarming trip.

What made this trip even more special was Abhishek's presence. During our 90-day stay in the U.S., his demanding work schedule meant he mostly had only weekends free to spend with us. *This Fourth of July holiday week* was a rare gift, offering the chance to travel together, unhurried and as a complete family. It felt precious, like an unexpected blessing at the perfect moment.

Reunion in Massachusetts and Boston: Friends and Family

Early that morning, Abhishek left at 8:45 a.m. to pick up our rental car: a Volkswagen Polo hatchback. By 9:40 a.m., he returned to find us already waiting in the lobby with our bags neatly packed, excitement buzzing in the air. Once we loaded everything into the car, it was filled to the brim. We were all set for a much-anticipated trip arranged by Neha and Abhishek; a journey that promised reunions, family time, and new memories.

We set off at 10 a.m. and drove non-stop towards *Grove Street, Massachusetts*, where we were scheduled to meet my veterinary batchmates; a smooth four-hour ride with Abhishek confidently at the wheel. Along the way, we enjoyed Neha's delicious homemade rolls; they were delightful. During the drive, I sent updates to Dr. Paul Chapin, Dr. Shama, and Dr. Gangadhar, my collegemates, all of whom were eagerly looking forward to our arrival.

We reached around 2:20 p.m. It was a joyous reunion; meeting after nearly 25 years. Neha and Sunitha were already familiar to them, and I proudly introduced them to Abhishek. They had prepared a wonderful spread of Indian snacks, sweets, and kebabs. The three of us Paul, Gangadhar and I enjoyed Scotch on the rocks, while the others chose beer or wine. We reminisced about our college days, shared stories, and laughter, and took several photographs to capture these precious moments.

After spending a cheerful few hours together, they suggested taking us out for dinner at a Thai restaurant. We had to politely decline, as we were scheduled to visit our cousin Harish in Boston that evening. After warm goodbyes, we left for *Boston*.

By 7 p.m., we reached Harish's home. It was truly wonderful to see him after such a long time. For dinner, he had thoughtfully ordered vegetarian dishes for Neha, Sunitha, and Abhishek, while he and I enjoyed some flavourful chicken.

He introduced me to a Japanese whisky called *Hibiki*. I was tasting it for the first time, and it surprised me with how extraordinary it was; especially with ice and a dash of water.

Finally, after a warm and satisfying visit, we said our goodnights and headed to our hotel, the *Hyatt Regency Boston*, which Neha and Abhishek had booked for our stay. After unpacking and freshening up, we settled in for a restful night's sleep, content and grateful for such a memorable day.

Boston Freedom Trail Hike

The next morning, the four of us left the Hyatt Regency and reached Harish's flat by 9 a.m. For breakfast, we enjoyed baked chocolate buns, and Harish made a fresh cup of coffee for me while the others had orange juice. He had also prepared perfectly done sunny-side-up eggs and delicious sandwiches with avocado, onions, and lime juice. It was a simple yet refreshing start to the day.

After eating, all five of us stepped out for a short stroll around his apartment complex. His flat was impressive; spotlessly clean, equipped with automated gadgets, and thoughtfully organized. From there, we walked to Wellington Station to catch the Orange

Line train, as Neha had planned our visit to the famous Freedom Trail.

The *Freedom Trail* is a 2.5-mile (4 km) path that connects sixteen historically significant sites. It begins at Boston Common in downtown Boston, continues past iconic landmarks such as the Old North Church and Paul Revere House, and ends at the Bunker Hill Monument in Charlestown. Along the way, visitors encounter graveyards, churches, museums, colonial-era buildings, and even a naval frigate.

Most sites are free or accept donations, while a few, like the Old South Meeting House, Old State House, and Paul Revere House, charge a nominal entry fee. The trail is beautifully marked throughout by a continuous *red-brick line.* Despite the hot and humid weather, we thoroughly enjoyed the walk. Midway, we took a break at the Sam Adams Downtown *Boston Taproom.* They stamped the backs of our hands and checked our IDs before serving us. We relaxed with some chilled beer and snacks before continuing the trail.

The official points along the trail include: *Boston Common, Massachusetts State House, Park Street Church, Granary Burying Ground, King's Chapel Burying Ground, Boston Latin School, Benjamin Franklin statue, Old Corner Bookstore, Old South Meeting House, Boston Massacre Site, Faneuil Hall, Paul Revere House, Old North Church, Copp's Hill Burying Ground, USS Constitution, and finally the Bunker Hill Monument.*

The USS *Constitution*, the historic naval frigate, looked magnificent. Visitors are allowed inside in timed batches, and entry is free. Unfortunately, we couldn't tour the interior because we were short on time; and, to my regret, I had forgotten to carry our passports, which are mandatory for entry.

During our trek, we also stopped at the famous *Mike's Pastry*, a place Neha had heard so much about. She chose two varieties; Limoncello and Boston cream pie, both were absolutely delicious. By the end of the walk, we were tired but happy. Though the trail was only 2.5 miles, the heat made it feel much longer. Still, it was a memorable experience, made even more special by Harish's cheerful company.

After finishing, we caught the Green Line train back to Harish's flat, freshened up, bid him goodbye, and returned to our hotel to check out before starting our drive to Maine. With hearts full from the laughter, stories, and historic streets of Boston, we set off toward Maine; eager for the natural beauty and adventures that awaited us at Acadia National Park.

Arrival in Maine - Acadia National Park Visit

We left Boston and began the four-hour drive to our *Airbnb, Creekside Crib, in Otis, Maine*, with Neha driving beautifully throughout the journey. She and Abhishek usually take turns during long-distance trips, but that evening and night she handled the entire stretch with calm confidence and ease.

We reached the Airbnb late at night and eased the car into our designated spot, grateful to finally stretch our legs. Inside, after a quick round of unpacking and freshening up, Neha and Abhishek, still running on the last traces of travel energy, whipped up a simple yet satisfying dinner. Ready-to-eat paneer and dal, paired with rice cooked in the microwave, came together in minutes. It wasn't elaborate, but in that quiet Maine night, the warm, homely flavours felt like the perfect reward after the long journey.

Our accommodation turned out to be an absolute delight. The hosts lived on the ground floor while we had the entire first floor to ourselves, complete with a private entrance.

The charming two-bedroom, one-bath unit was cozy, clean, well-equipped, and had reliable Wi-Fi; ideal for our four-day stay. The main bedroom featured a comfortable queen-sized bed, a streaming TV with Netflix and Hulu, and a table with seating for four. The second room served as a lounge with another TV, a kitchenette stocked with a mini-fridge, microwave, toaster oven, and essential utensils, along with a pull-out couch with a full-sized mattress. The bathroom had a neat single-person shower.

The property's surroundings were serene: lush vegetable and flower gardens, two beehives in the backyard, and a peaceful *Creekside loop trail* that we explored on our final day. Outside, a screened canopy tent with cushioned chairs and a gas grill made for lovely evening relaxation, which we enjoyed on alternate nights. The hosts owned a friendly hound dog named *Monet,* though we never happened to see him.

What truly elevated our stay were the homemade continental breakfast items our host had stocked in the room; many prepared with fresh local Maine produce, and some even harvested from the hosts' own garden. Each morning was a small celebration of the region's flavours.

We enjoyed *spinach quiche, oatmeal protein bars, Maine blueberry cinnamon muffins, berry yogurt parfaits, and French toast sticks served with local maple syrup*. There was also Honey Nut cereal and a selection of fresh fruits, with only the hot coffee left for us to prepare in the kitchenette. There was more than enough to begin each day on a wholesome and heartwarming note.

We made sure to respect the hosts' quiet hours from 10 p.m. to 5 a.m., and overall, our stay at Creekside Crib was peaceful, comfortable, and truly memorable; an ideal base for exploring Acadia National Park.

Day 1 - Acadia National Park: *Ocean Path Trail*

We woke up early, freshened up, and enjoyed the delicious homemade breakfast thoughtfully stocked by our Airbnb hosts. After packing some extra snacks, juice, and water, we set off for our first day of *trekking in Acadia National Park*. Because it was the Fourth of July holiday weekend, parking was extremely challenging, but after some patient searching, we finally found a spot and began our adventure.

Our first trek was the *Ocean Path Trail*, and it was wonderful. All four of us initially walked to the edge of the cliffs and sat on the rocks, watching the mighty Atlantic waves crash against the rugged shore below. The sight and sound were mesmerizing. We clicked several photos before Abhishek and Neha set off toward the more challenging *Beehive and Jordan Cliffs Trails*, which involved climbing iron rungs and ladders up steep cliff faces. Sunitha and I decided to take the gentler route, far better suited for us.

The Ocean Path Trail we chose, located on Mount Desert Island, is among Acadia's most popular treks: a mostly flat 2.2-mile coastal walk running from Sand Beach to Otter Point, parallel to the Park Loop Road where we had parked.

Along the way, we encountered hundreds of fellow visitors and local families enjoying the holiday week. Many smiled as they passed, and a few even stopped to chat, asking where we were from. Some asked us for directions too; thankfully, I had downloaded a map of the trail beforehand. A kind couple, noticing Sunitha and me taking individual photos of each other, offered to click a few of all of us together: a truly heart-warming gesture. I happily returned the favour and took photos for them as well.

The Ocean Path offers stunning views of *Sand Beach*, the rough and jagged Atlantic shoreline, Thunder Hole, and the majestic Otter Cliffs. Though generally easy, the trail becomes slightly uneven and slippery as it nears Otter Point. From the Sand Beach Overlook, we continued toward *Thunder Hole*, stopping often for photographs. Walking down the steps there, we could clearly hear the ocean rushing into the narrow cove, creating a deep booming sound: just like thunder, true to its name.

We then continued onward, bravely making our way to the *Otter Point Overlook*, the highest and most scenic viewpoint of the trail. The views were spectacular, with several hikers scattered around, soaking in the same breathtaking scenes. At one point, I even noticed a lone climber expertly making his way down the rocky cliff using professional gear: a striking sight against the vast ocean backdrop.

After spending some time enjoying the panorama, we walked back toward Sand Beach to wait for Neha and Abhishek, whose challenging trek ended at the same point. Once they returned, they waded into the chilly water and enjoyed the refreshing waves for about twenty minutes before we finally headed back to the car. After a short snack break, we told Neha and Abhishek that Thunder Hole was truly worth a visit, so they went ahead for a quick look while Sunitha and I relaxed in the car.

We then began driving toward *Echo Lake Beach*, as Neha wanted us to see its famous lighthouse. However, the approach road turned out to be extremely rocky and difficult. Only Neha and Abhishek continued ahead over the rough stretch for a closer look, while we stayed back halfway once the path became too tough. After taking a few photos, we continued driving to a viewpoint at the top of a nearby mountain, which offered a wonderfully scenic route on the way down.

By evening, we headed back to our Airbnb: tired, yet truly happy after such a beautiful first day at Acadia National Park. After freshening up, we spent a few peaceful moments chatting and sipping cider inside the *beautifully lit screened tent* in the front yard of our Airbnb. The clear night sky above was sprinkled with stars, and the entire garden glowing with hundreds of *fireflies*. It felt magical: almost like a dream.

Later, we returned inside for dinner and settled in for a restful night. With hearts full of awe and the soothing sounds of the Atlantic still echoing in our minds, we drifted off to sleep, eager for the adventures awaiting us the next day at Acadia.

Day 2 - Sunrise at Cadillac Mountain and Exploring Acadia National Park

Today, Neha and Abhishek had planned something truly special for us; *watching the sunrise from Cadillac Mountain.* Since we had to be there by 4 a.m., we woke up at 2 a.m., bundled ourselves in warm clothes to face the early-morning cold, and left our Airbnb in complete darkness. As it was far too early for breakfast, we packed the homemade items provided by our Airbnb host and carried them with us, along with water and some cool drinks. Neha and Abhishek had already printed our entry tickets to Cadillac Mountains; both for the car and for all four of us, as these needed to be shown at the entrance gate.

Cadillac Mountain, we were told is the highest peak on the North Atlantic seaboard, rising to 1,530 feet within Acadia National Park, Maine. Its summit offers sweeping views of the surrounding landscape, rugged coastline, and scattered offshore islands. For much of the year, *Cadillac Mountain is famously the first place in the United States to witness the sunrise.*

Neha informed us that access during peak season is limited, with only 55 cars allowed each day, making a vehicle reservation essential. Thankfully, she had booked ours well in advance; one of her signature, well-planned touches.

We drove up the winding Cadillac Summit Road through layers of mist and fog. When we reached the parking area a little before 4 a.m., we noticed several cars already parked. A short walk brought us to the summit, where around thirty people were waiting quietly in the cold darkness. We found a comfortable spot and sat down, hoping the mist would clear in time for sunrise. And we were so lucky; it did.

Just before sunrise, the sky began to clear, revealing a soft, mesmerizing glow that seemed almost magical. At 4:23 a.m., the first hints of orange and yellow spread across the horizon, slowly igniting the vast landscape below.

By 4:53 a.m., the sun burst forth in brilliant, fiery colours, painting the sky in a spectacle so breathtaking it left us momentarily speechless. Standing here, one doesn't just watch dawn break: one feels the day being born.

The moment was spellbinding, filling us with awe, and instantly reminding us of the sunrise we once witnessed near a volcano in Bali, Indonesia. We lingered for another hour on the summit, drinking in the sweeping views in silence, while *Sunitha found a quiet corner to sit for a brief, meditative pause.* A small signboard reminded us that this is a sacred place for the Wabanaki people, who call it *"Wapuwoc": the White Mountain of First Light.* Standing there, witnessing nature's grandeur unfold, we truly understood why.

Afterwards, we headed to the *Wild Gardens of Acadia, the Nature Center, and the Abbe Museum.* With the park still quiet and nothing yet open, we wandered lazily, soaking in the crisp morning air, before returning to the car, where all four of us dozed off for a while, laughing at ourselves afterward. We then enjoyed our homemade breakfast and washed it down with some cool drinks, feeling rested and ready for the day's adventures.

When the Wild Gardens finally opened, we began exploring in earnest. The gardens showcase over 400 native plant species, every turn revealed delicate wildflowers, ferns, and mosses, and the peaceful atmosphere felt almost meditative.

From the gardens, we set off on the *Jesup Path-Hemlock Path loop*, a 1.5 miles easy-to-moderate trail that felt like stepping into another world. A boardwalk carried us over quiet wetlands, tall birch trees towered overhead, and the serene hemlock forests created a canopy of calm. Interpretive signs, benches, and wide, smooth boardwalks made the trail inviting at every step.

Along the way, we were delighted to spot a *porcupine* contentedly munching on vegetation, seemingly unaware of the visitors nearby, and a pair of nimble *red squirrels* darting energetically among the trees. The gentle sounds of rustling leaves and chirping birds filled the air with life and magic.

Next, we drove to the *Hulls Cove Visitor Center*, parked the car, and went inside to gather guidance about hikes within Acadia National Park. We picked up maps, checked bus schedules, and decided to catch Bus No. 5 to Jordan Pond, a scenic ride of about twenty minutes.

Once there, we first wandered along a short trail on the historic *Carriage Road*, a picturesque stretch lined with flowing streams, charming stone bridges, and lush, towering trees.

The gentle sounds of water and rustling leaves created a serene backdrop, setting the tone for the afternoon.

Afterwards, we made our way to the restaurant *Jordan Pond House* and booked a table for four. Within about twenty-five minutes, we were seated and indulged in a delicious lunch, including their famous *Popovers,* a classic American pastry that was light, airy, and utterly satisfying.

Following lunch, we embarked on a leisurely walk around *Jordan Pond*, a stunningly beautiful waterbody. Though called a "pond," it resembled a large, pristine lake, with crystal-clear waters reflecting the surrounding mountains. We paused frequently for photographs, marvelling at the clarity of the water, the vibrant greenery, and the quiet majesty of the landscape.

By evening, we caught Bus No. 5 back to the Visitor Center. The trail around Jordan Pond is a more demanding hike, with rugged terrain, and Neha reminded us that it would take several hours: far more than we had the energy for after starting our day at 2 a.m. We decided to save it for the next day.

Tired but happy, we drove back to our Airbnb, freshened up, and relaxed while Neha and Abhishek discussed plans for tomorrow. It had been a long day, yet one filled with unforgettable beauty; nature at its absolute best.

As night fell, the serenity of the forest and the gentle sounds of the creek reminded us that some of life's most treasured moments are those spent in quiet awe of the world around us.

Day 3 - The Jordan Pond Loop Challenge and The Magic of Bar Island

We woke up a little leisurely today, enjoyed a hearty breakfast, and drove to the Visitor Center. From there, we caught the bus to Jordan Pond, ready to tackle the much-awaited trek. The loop spans nearly 3.3 miles, and it took us a good three hours to complete.

Jordan Pond is one of Acadia's most iconic landscapes: a crystal-clear pond nestled in a steep valley carved long ago by retreating glaciers, as we learned. It is framed by the beautiful Penobscot and Pemetic Mountains, creating a breathtaking view that feels almost like a painting. Along the way, we listened for the haunting calls of common loons, spotted signs of beaver activity, and even scanned the granite cliffs for nesting falcons.

The *Jordan Pond Path* is popular: and with good reason. The eastern half is easy, flat, and scenic, featuring a mix of gravel, boardwalks, and gentle shoreline; perfect for soaking in the views. The western half, however, is rocky, uneven, and far more challenging. Rangers often recommend starting with the eastern side so visitors can turn back if the western section proves too difficult.

As we made our way around the loop, we noticed several people turning back at the rocky sections. Some stretches allowed only one person at a time, requiring careful balance along the uneven stones, and one section demanded using both hands to scramble over massive boulders. In the trickiest and narrowest spots, the four of us held hands, cheering and encouraging one another with a mix of laughter and determination.

With perseverance and plenty of camaraderie, we completed the full loop. When we finally returned to our starting point, we were exhausted but triumphant; proud to have completed the challenging hike. It had been tough, indeed, yet immensely rewarding.

After the long trek, as we made our way back, we saw streams of visitors heading toward the historic Jordan Pond House for their famed popovers: a tradition as beloved as the landscape itself. The cozy white cottage, with its lawn overlooking the pond and mountains, looked every bit the perfect place to unwind.

We smiled, remembering our own visit the previous afternoon, when we lingered over warm popovers and tea, soaking in the view. But the day was far from over; another adventure awaited us, and our next destination: Bar Island, promised something entirely different.

Bar Island: A Walk Across the Ocean Floor

Our next stop was the enchanting Bar Harbor area of Acadia National Park, where nature puts on a rare spectacle. At low tide, an exposed gravel bar emerges between the mainland and Bar Island, creating a temporary pathway that vanishes with the returning tide. For about 1.5 hours around low tide, the flat walkway lies fully exposed, flanked by glistening water. Small tide pools reveal miniature marine worlds, while the sparkling expanse of Frenchman Bay stretches endlessly around us, creating a surreal, almost mystical landscape.

Crossing the bar, we marvelled at the rocks covered with barnacles and long strands of seaweed: simple reminders that just hours earlier, this entire stretch had been underwater. Once on Bar Island, the trail gradually ascends through forested paths along an old road, eventually opening to breathtaking viewpoints overlooking Bar Harbor. The 1.9-mile round trip takes you over rocky terrain, sand, gravel, and forested trails; each step feels like an adventure in itself.

We paused often to capture the extraordinary beauty around us, savouring the fleeting sense of stepping into a secret world destined to disappear with the tide.

On the way back, we took turns skimming flat stones across the water, just as we had in childhood, counting how many times each stone leapt before sinking. A stark warning posted for visitors added a thrill to our exploration: ***"If you lose track of time and get stranded on the island, it will be nine hours before the bar reappears."*** It was a reminder that here, nature holds all the power, and we were fortunate guests in its rhythm.

After returning to the mainland, we planned to explore the town, stroll through its charming streets, and soak in the lively atmosphere before heading back just in time for high tide, eager to witness the island's complete transformation.

Lunch and The Historic Shore Path

Hunger led us to *Melt*, a restaurant famous for its delicious sandwiches. We each ordered hearty sandwiches with fries; the meal was yummy, filling, and absolutely perfect after the long trek. We then set out for the *Friends of the Shore Path*, a century-old 1.5-mile coastal walkway lined with charming homes, elegant hotels, and beautifully maintained gardens. Although badly damaged in the storms of 2024, it has since been wonderfully restored.

Along the path, we came across the famous *Balance Rock*, a massive glacial erratic carried from near Bangor by ancient glaciers and deposited here more than 10,000 years ago. Neha and Abhishek couldn't resist the playful challenge of giving it a shove, straining and laughing as if they could somehow budge this prehistoric giant. Of course, the rock didn't move an inch; but we preserved the moment with some fantastic photos of their valiant (and hilarious) attempt, making it a memory we would treasure forever.

High Tide Magic - The Disappearing Bar

To complete the experience, we returned to see Bar Island at high tide; and what a sight it was. *The entire gravel bar had vanished beneath the water.* Where we had walked just a few hours earlier, there now stretched a wide expanse of ocean, leaving the island completely cut off, just as predicted. Nature never ceases to amaze. Later I merged videos of our low-tide walk with the high-tide scene, and the contrast is astonishing; you can literally watch the landscape reshape itself within hours. It's no wonder this place is protected as part of a national park.

We are truly grateful to Neha and Abhishek, who research everything so thoroughly and take us to such unique, memorable places. With our hearts full and our feet tired, we took the bus back to the Visitor Center, retrieved our car, and drove toward the Airbnb, stopping en route for a hearty dinner. A wonderful end to an incredible day.

As we drove back to Creekside Crib, the sun dipped low over the mountains, casting golden hues across the glistening waters. We felt a profound sense of accomplishment: not just from conquering the challenging Jordan Pond Loop, but from being present in such awe-inspiring landscapes, witnessing the playful rhythms of nature at Bar Island, and sharing laughter, stories, and quiet moments together.

The day had tested our endurance, yet it rewarded us with memories that will linger forever: the magic of Acadia, the power of the tides, and the joy of exploring it all as a family. By the time we reached our cozy Airbnb, tired yet elated, we knew that this day would remain etched in our hearts long after the mountains and ponds faded from view.

Day 4 – The Quiet Beauty of Schoodic Point

Today, Neha planned something special and far less crowded: a visit to *Schoodic Point on the Schoodic Peninsula*, a serene and lesser-known part of Acadia National Park. The peninsula lies about four miles east of Bar Harbor and makes up only around

5% of Acadia, including the towns of Gouldsboro and Winter Harbor. Remarkably, it is visited by barely 0.4% of all Acadia visitors; shocking; but true. Thanks to Neha and Abhishek's thorough research, we were fortunate to experience this hidden gem.

Often called the quiet side of Acadia, Schoodic Point boasts a rugged coastline, dramatic Atlantic views, and nearly empty trails, offering a peaceful contrast to the bustling crowds of Mount Desert Island. From here, the views of Cadillac Mountain are spectacular, and the pounding surf against the rocks is utterly mesmerizing.

Our first stop was a beautiful picnic area with neatly placed tables and benches. Only two other families were around, giving the place an untouched, tranquil feel. There is a lovely bridge here over the peninsula, and we saw two people casually fishing while several boats glided across the water. We walked along the bridge, enjoying the cool breeze, spotting birds, and capturing plenty of pictures of the serene surroundings.

Later we drove along the *Scenic Loop Road*, which winds gracefully around the peninsula. Stopping at one of the rocky shore access points, we climbed down to the water's edge to watch the waves crash dramatically against the granite cliffs. The raw, rugged beauty of the shoreline was breathtaking.

Next, we headed to the *Sundew Trail*, a short 0.7 mile nature loop located on the *Schoodic Education and Research Center campus*. The trail winds through dense forest near the coastline and forms part of ongoing ecological research. Many plants, shrubs, and trees had labelled markers explaining their significance.

This trail was rougher than expected, and yes, full of mosquitoes. Thankfully, Neha and Abhishek had ensured we used insect repellent sprays from Day 1, so we were well prepared. At the end of the trail, we reached a rugged rocky shoreline where we spent some quiet moments soaking in the untouched natural beauty.

Interestingly, we hardly saw any other visitors here, very unusual compared to the rest of Acadia, where crowds of tourists, families, and hikers are common. Throughout our trip, we had interacted with several friendly families who offered to take our pictures and asked where we were from. But here at Schoodic, it felt like we had the entire place to ourselves. Due to the national holiday, the research campus was closed, but the visit was still fabulous; a peaceful, remote corner of Acadia that was calm, beautiful, and incredibly memorable.

As we drove back to Creekside Crib, the quiet beauty of Schoodic Point lingered in our minds: the endless horizon, the waves crashing against the cliffs, and the sense of being completely alone with nature. It was a rare moment of stillness in a week full of adventure, a reminder that sometimes the most memorable experiences are the simplest and most serene.

That evening, under a canopy of stars and the gentle hum of the forest, we felt deeply grateful for the tranquillity, the laughter shared, and the magic of discovering a hidden corner of Acadia all to ourselves.

Day of Departure from Acadia: Goodbye to the Mountains, Hello Harvard

The next morning, we freshened up, enjoyed our breakfast: savouring the last of the lovely delicacies, and packed our bags to check out of the Airbnb, taking care to leave the place just as neat as when we arrived. For the first time since our stay began, we met the owner as he tended to his beautiful vegetable and flower garden. He greeted us warmly and even offered some freshly harvested organic peas: sweet, crisp, and absolutely delicious.

We thanked him for the wonderfully comfortable stay and the wholesome homemade breakfast items he had provided each day. Before leaving, he suggested we take the one-mile trail that begins right behind the house and leads to a scenic stream. We followed his advice, and the trail was peaceful and lovely, though certainly alive with mosquitoes. After the short walk, we returned to the car, loaded our luggage, and bid a fond farewell to our charming Creekside Crib Airbnb and to Acadia National Park, which had gifted us so many unforgettable memories.

Neha and Abhishek had one final highlight planned before heading home: a visit to *Harvard University in Cambridge,* Massachusetts. Founded in 1636, Harvard is, we learnt, the oldest institution of higher learning in the United States, renowned for its academic excellence, historic campus, and the world's largest academic library system.

After a smooth four-hour drive from Acadia, we arrived at Harvard, where our cousin Harish was already waiting. We had called him a day earlier to join us, and it was lovely to have him along again as we explored one of the world's most prestigious universities. Neha and Abhishek had planned a campus walking tour. We first checked at the reception desk for a guided tour, but the timings didn't suit our schedule. Abhishek quickly downloaded the official Harvard app and became our guide for the day.

The self-guided walking tour, Abhishek informed us, covered fourteen mapped stops across *Harvard Yard*, including the *John Harvard Statue, Widener Library, Memorial Hall, the Science Center*, and the *Harvard Lampoon building*.

The walk spans about a mile and takes roughly forty-five to sixty minutes, offering clear insights into Harvard's history, architecture, and student life.

We strolled through the iconic Harvard Yard, admired the grand Memorial Church, gazed at the Lowell Bell Tower, and absorbed the vibrant blend of tradition and youthful energy across the campus. It was a pleasant and informative visit, and we felt genuinely happy to wander a place we had previously known only through books and films.

After the tour, we went to *Saloniki Greek*, a lovely restaurant nearby that Harish recommended from an earlier visit. The Greek beer was refreshing, and the meal was both delicious and satisfying: just what we needed after the long walk. Once we finished, we said goodbye to Harish as he boarded a train back to Boston.

The four of us then began the long five-hour drive back to New Jersey. Not long after we set off, while twilight still lingered, we spotted a fox walking along the wooded roadside: a brief but delightful surprise. The rest of the journey passed in conversation as we spoke about the grand finale awaiting us the next day: the Fourth of July fireworks.

We finally reached the flat around 2 a.m., exhausted yet content after such a memorable trip. After freshening up, we went to sleep, grateful for the experiences we had shared and for Neha and Abhishek's thoughtful planning.

As we drifted off, memories of Acadia's rugged cliffs, serene waters, and hidden trails blended seamlessly with the vibrant atmosphere of Harvard's historic campus. This leg of our journey had been a perfect balance of nature, history, and family: a reminder that the best adventures are those shared with loved ones and crafted with care.

The mountains, the ponds, the islands, and the campus would linger in our hearts long after the journey ended, a testament to discovery, togetherness, and the quiet joy of exploring both the world and the bonds within it.

DAY OF CELEBRATION: 4TH OF JULY

A SPECTACULAR FINALE TO AN AWESOME HOLIDAY

Day of Celebration: 4th of July-A Spectacular Finale to an Awesome Holiday

"The most memorable journeys are not measured by miles, but by moments shared and hearts touched."

We woke up a little late today; after all, it was the *Fourth of July, America's National Day*, when the entire country bursts into colour, celebration, and patriotic cheer. Our aunt Gayathri was arriving to stay with us for two days, so the morning passed joyfully as we prepared a variety of dishes, filling the home with familiar aromas and the anticipation of a festive evening.

After lunch, we stepped out to shop for fresh fruits, vegetables, and essentials, restocking the pantry after our week-long holiday. Later, we drove to pick up Gayathri aunty from her relatives' place and returned home, excited for the grand finale of our trip.

By evening, the five of us set out for *Liberty State Park*, where we planned to watch the *Fourth of July fireworks.* Neha and Abhishek had thoughtfully packed sandwiches, cool drinks, a chair, a stool, and a large mat for our picnic on the lawns.

Abhishek dropped us as close to the entrance as possible and then drove off to park the car far away, well aware that after the fireworks, the entire area would turn into a sea of traffic. He soon zipped back to us on his electric scooter, smiling triumphantly.

As we walked toward the Hudson River waterfront, the breathtaking panorama unfolded: the Statue of Liberty standing tall before us, her silhouette glowing in the evening light, while the glittering New York skyline stretched across the river like a jewelled crown. The atmosphere was electric.

Abhishek and Neha explained that the Fourth of July fireworks can be viewed from many locations around the region. Some prefer Jersey City's Exchange Place for its clear views of Manhattan's skyline and the East River fireworks. But others like us, choose Liberty State Park for its sweeping, unobstructed views of the Statue of Liberty, Ellis Island, and the multiple fireworks shows that erupt across both New York and New Jersey.

When we arrived around 8 p.m., the Army band was already performing with tremendous energy. Police and security officers were everywhere: on foot, on horseback, in patrol cars, patrolling the river by boat, and even hovering in the sky. The sense of scale and organization was astonishing.

By 9 p.m., thousands of families had gathered on the lawns. Picnics sprawled across blankets, children ran around waving glow sticks, and music played in the background as one of the region's largest Independence Day celebrations came alive.

Neha and Abhishek had chosen the perfect viewing spot, right at the edge of the lawn near the riverbank. The moment the fireworks began, the sky erupted into a riot of colours. From where we sat, we could see four to five displays at once; three from New Jersey and two from New York and Brooklyn. The most spectacular, however, were the New York and New Jersey shows directly across from us, dominating the skyline with their grandeur. The night sky glowed with crimson bursts, golden cascades, sparkling spirals, and shimmering fountains that seemed to paint the entire horizon with light.

Each burst was more dazzling than the last. The crowd gasped, cheered, and applauded as the sky turned into a living canvas of fire and magic. For several unforgettable minutes, the world felt suspended: just light, sound, and pure joy. We were truly fortunate to witness such a spectacular display.

While enjoying the show, we savoured the sandwiches and cool drinks Neha and Abhishek had lovingly packed. When the fireworks finally came to an end, we joined the enormous crowd slowly making its way toward the exit, the roads overflowing with cars and people. Abhishek left on his electric scooter to retrieve the car, while we continued walking with the steady stream of spectators.

At one point, as we were walking out of the park, the police halted all movement; both vehicles and pedestrians, to let a Light Rail train pass. The sudden stillness, the entire crowd frozen in place, and the lone train gliding quietly through created an unexpectedly comic moment amid the chaos.

After walking a long distance away from the congested area, we spotted Abhishek waiting with the car, his timing perfect as always. We drove home tired but exhilarated, our hearts still glowing from the night's magic. Back at the flat, we freshened up, enjoyed the delicious dinner we had prepared earlier, chatted for a while, and finally drifted off to sleep; hearts full and spirits soaring.

It was, without doubt, a spectacular finale to an unforgettable holiday: a celebration of togetherness, gratitude, and the joy of experiencing America's grandest tradition under a sky full of fireworks.

Reflections on a Week of Celebration

Our Fourth of July week felt like the perfect symphony of celebration, exploration, and family togetherness. It began with our joyful reunion in Massachusetts and Boston, followed by the serene drive to Maine and our stay at the charming Creekside Crib in Otis.

We immersed ourselves in the breathtaking beauty of Acadia National Park: watching sunrises paint the sky from Cadillac Mountain, wandering scenic trails, exploring lush gardens, and savouring leisurely homemade breakfasts. Each day was a gift: stunning landscapes, quiet reflections, meaningful conversations, and the simple joy of being together.

Evenings were spent cooking, chatting, and soaking in the calm of our surroundings. Each moment felt like a gentle reminder that the most precious parts of travel are the shared experiences and joyful moments that linger long after the journey ends. As the week drew to its close, the grand Fourth of July celebrations became the crowning highlight.

Welcoming Gayathri aunty, preparing a vibrant feast together, shopping for fresh produce, picnicking along the Hudson River, and witnessing fireworks that lit up the New

York and New Jersey skies made the day utterly unforgettable: a spectacular crescendo to an already extraordinary week.

Looking back, it wasn't merely the places we visited that made this week special, but the warmth, the shared smiles, and the love woven through each day. It renewed our spirits, strengthened our bonds, and became a joyful celebration; not just of Independence Day, but of family, togetherness, and life's simplest blessings.

After a few days of rest at Neha's home, we found ourselves eagerly awaiting with bated breath, our next adventure; a warm reunion with relatives in Ashburn, Virginia, and the sightseeing in Washington, D.C., that we had missed during our 18-day East and West Coast tour due to the rains.

"A week of adventures may end, but the love, joy, and memories we shared will illuminate our hearts forever."

– Narayan Pratap

WARM REUNION IN WASHINGTON, D.C., AND VIRGINIA

EXPLORING WASHINGTON, D.C., AND FAMILY TIME

CHAPTER 9

A WARM REUNION IN WASHINGTON, D.C., AND VIRGINIA

"Family is the compass that guides us, the roots that ground us, and the wings that help us rise. Every journey feels complete when shared with them."

We left Neha's flat at 3:30 p.m., catching a bus to Journal Square before boarding the PATH train to 33rd Street in New York. From there, we walked to our pickup point for the long-distance bus to Virginia, where we were headed to visit our dear cousins, Ksheeraja and Ansari. After wishing us goodbye, Neha returned home, and we settled into our seats for the four-hour ride. The journey was smooth and pleasant, with lovely views unfolding along the way; small towns, wooded stretches, and evening lights glowing as dusk slowly settled.

We reached *Vienna, Virginia,* around 9:15 p.m., where Ansari was waiting with a warm smile and an even warmer hug.

After greeting us, he led us to his beautiful car, and we drove about 45 minutes to their home in *Ashburn*. Once there, we freshened up and spent time chatting with Ansari, Ksheeraja, her mother Radhika, and their younger daughter, Tania. The comfort of family conversations after a long trip felt wonderful.

Later, I enjoyed a couple of pegs of Blue Label whisky, followed by a delicious dinner of homemade mutton biryani with Ansari; rich, flavourful, and perfect after a day of travel. Then they took us on a tour of their stunning home, and we were amazed by the artistry on display. Much of the woodwork: sofas, tables, and counters, had been painstakingly handcrafted by Ansari himself. The interiors, beautifully coordinated in soothing shades of blue and white, reflected Ksheeraja's impeccable taste. Ansari even took me down to the basement to show his full-fledged workshop, a treasure trove of state-of-the-art carpentry tools where creativity and craftsmanship clearly came alive.

The exterior was just as charming: lovely gardens, a manicured lawn, a peaceful backyard, and a welcoming front porch surrounded by trees. It felt like a serene retreat tucked away in Virginia's quiet suburbs. We chatted late into the night before finally calling it a day, grateful for the warmth, hospitality, and joy of being with family.

Exploring Washington, D.C. – Capitol Grandeur and Museum Wonders

We woke up around 8:30 a.m. to a refreshing start. After a wash, Ksheeraja offered us hot ginger water followed by her lovely tea. Breakfast was a comforting spread of idli, chutney, and sambar;

simple yet perfect before a day of sightseeing. Once ready, she drove us to the *Ashburn Metro Station*. Suni and I purchased one-day metro passes and boarded the Silver Line from Ashburn to *Capitol South Station*. After alighting, we walked about nine minutes to the *Capitol Visitor Center*, where Neha had booked our 1 p.m. tour.

Entry to the *U.S. Capitol* is free, but visitors must pre-book a time slot. We joined the queue, had our tickets checked, and received our visitor stickers. The tour began with a 13-minute introductory film on the construction and significance of the Capitol Building: a remarkable insight into its history and symbolism. Afterwards, a guide handed us audio devices and led us through the grand interiors. The architecture, artwork, and sheer sense of history made the Capitol truly breathtaking. Among the original works are pieces depicting Benjamin Franklin, John Fitch, Robert Fulton, and events such as the Cession of Louisiana. The walls are also adorned with animals, insects, and natural flora indigenous to the United States.

The guide pointed out a compass star inlaid in the floor, marking the exact point where *Washington, D.C., is divided into its four quadrants* and serving as the reference for how all addresses in the city are designated (NE, NW, SE, or SW). Our guide was an amazing person who shared a wealth of information with us. One section of the building features huge statues of leading personalities representing the 50 states of the USA.

Neha had advised us not to exit after the Capitol visit but to continue through the connecting tunnel to the entrance of the *Jefferson Building of the Library of Congress*. Although we couldn't scan the QR code required for entry, a kind security guard assisted us by printing two tickets. The library was magnificent; vast, ornate, and absolutely worth the visit.

From there, we returned to the Capitol South Metro Station and took the Silver Line again, this time getting off at *Smithsonian*. A short seven-minute walk brought us to the *Museum of Natural History*. Before going inside, we refreshed ourselves with lemonade and burgers at a nearby eatery.

The museum was a delight; ancient mammals, dinosaurs, aquatic life, human evolution exhibits: each section was mesmerizing. One of the most wonderful aspects of Washington, D.C., is that *most museums offer free entry*. While some require timed passes, walk-ins are usually allowed, making the experience accessible and enjoyable. After finishing our museum visit, we returned to the *Smithsonian Metro Station*, took the Silver Line all the way back to Ashburn, and got down at the last stop. Tania arrived to pick us up and drive us back home.

That night, we joined Ksheeraja and Ansari at a party hosted by Aruna, a close friend from their MBA days in Bangalore who, back then, often visited us on weekends. Meeting Aruna and her husband after nearly 25 years filled us with nostalgia. The gathering was lively; warm hosts, wonderful conversations, and a friendly group who made us feel instantly at home. Aruna's daughter, training to be a professional bartender, crafted delicious cocktails for everyone. The table was overflowing with food, as each couple had brought a dish, making it a true potluck celebration.

Back home later that night, we learned that Ksheeraja and Ansari were preparing for their elder daughter's upcoming engagement ceremony. Ansari was busy building a new bar counter and dining table, with the theme set to be an elegant all-white décor. His craftsmanship was truly impressive. Even amidst all the work, the house felt full of joy, warmth, and shared excitement. It was only when we glanced at the clock and saw it was nearly 3 a.m. that we realized how quickly time had passed. With hearts full and spirits high, we finally called it a night.

Family Time, Farewells, and the Journey Back

We woke up late this morning and began the day with steaming cups of tea. Radhika Aunty treated us to crispy, golden dosas for breakfast, while Ksheeraja prepared a sumptuous mutton biryani for lunch, which we relished wholeheartedly.

In the afternoon, we joined her for a walk along the beautiful trail behind their house, winding our way through nearly three to four kilometres of serene greenery, soaking in the fresh air and tranquil surroundings.

During our stay in Ashburn, we cherished every moment spent with family. Mornings were filled with laughter over breakfast, casual chats, and small neighbourhood adventures, while afternoons and evenings were devoted to helping with the preparations for their elder daughter's engagement.

From watching Ansari work his carpentry magic on the new bar counter and dining table, to seeing Ksheeraja and Tania decorating and draping, we felt fully immersed in the joyous energy of a family coming together. It was more than just a visit, it was bonding, sharing stories, learning family traditions, and celebrating love, care, and togetherness. Every moment left us with lasting memories and a deep appreciation for the warmth and hospitality of our cousins.

The next day, after a hearty breakfast, we packed our bags and expressed our heartfelt thanks to Ansari, Ksheeraja, and Radhika Aunty for the wonderful time we had spent in their company. We regretted not bidding a proper goodbye to Tania, who was engrossed in creating a backdrop painting to welcome Arshia and David for their upcoming engagement.

Ksheeraja and Radhika Aunty then drove us, along with our luggage, to meet another cousin of Sunitha; Ram Laxmi, and her husband Venkat, who had kindly invited us for lunch. We spent a few delightful hours catching up; they had been our next-door neighbours in Bangalore two decades ago. The meal was warm and memorable, and their friendliness made the reunion all the more special.

After lunch, we thanked Ram Laxmi and Venkat for their warm hospitality and set off in their car to Vienna to visit another of Sunitha's relatives, Thammu, uncle, and his wife. We spent a short time with them, enjoyed tea and a lively chat before reluctantly preparing to leave again, aware that our bus to New York City would be arriving soon.

Riding in Venkat's car, we watched the familiar streets pass by, feeling a mix of nostalgia and gratitude for the time spent reconnecting with family. As we reached the bus station and bid him farewell, our hearts were full, carrying the warmth and memories of a truly memorable visit. The bus arrived at 5:45 p.m., and we set off non-stop for New York City, a four-hour journey.

Neha and Abhishek were there to welcome us at the bus stop and took us to a popular spot called *Supreme Pizza* for dinner. We sampled five varieties; White Garlic, Upside-Down, Cheese, Hot Honey, and Chicken Parm, each one delicious and utterly satisfying.

After dinner, we strolled back and caught the PATH train from New York City to Journal Square Station in New Jersey.

Feeling pleasantly full, we decided to walk the rest of the way home. Once back, we freshened up and turned in for the night, leaving the task of unpacking our bags for the next day.

Reflection and Reminiscences

Travel, at its heart, is not only about places; it is about people. Our days in Washington, D.C. and Virginia reminded us that journeys become meaningful when they bring us closer to those we love.

Between the grandeur of the Capitol, the majesty of the museums, and the buzzing metro rides, it was the warmth waiting for us at the end of each day: hot meals, familiar laughter, handmade furniture crafted with love and unhurried conversations; that truly defined this chapter.

In the midst of busy sightseeing and lively gatherings, we rediscovered the quiet joy of being welcomed like family, embraced by memories old and new.

As we travelled back to New York, our bags were heavier but our hearts were even fuller. The late-night chats, the long walks, the aroma of biryani, the creative chaos of engagement preparations, and the reunion with friends after 25 years; all blended into a mosaic of cherished moments.

Some journeys leave you with photographs, others with stories; this one left us with both, and with the beautiful reassurance that no matter how far we wander, family has a way of making every destination feel like home.

CHAPTER 10

A TAPESTRY OF NINETY DAYS AND THE JOY OF COMING HOME

"Travel is more than the seeing of sights; it is a change that goes on, deep and permanent, in the ideas of living."

– Miriam Beard

As the journey drew to a close, memories overflowed: of people, places, shared moments, and quiet joys. This trip had been far more than sightseeing; it was a celebration of life, family, and discovery. Reflecting on the past ninety days felt almost surreal. Three months filled with wonder, warmth, and a kaleidoscope of experiences across the United States had gently come to an end.

From the bustling streets of New York to the serene beauty of Jordan Pond and the gentle sunrise over Cadillac Mountain in

Acadia National Park, from the dazzling lights of Las Vegas to the shifting tides at Bar Island: each day felt like a page in a story that will stay with me forever.

Our journey began in New Jersey, where everyday pleasures blended seamlessly with exploration: wandering through towns and cities, watching cherry blossoms bloom, picking strawberries, enjoying a shooting adventure, visiting Bear Mountain, playing Monster Golf, and celebrating Mother's Day with a memorable brunch. In New York City, we explored four of the five boroughs and embarked on a walking food tour, tasting flavours from around the world while absorbing the city's unmistakable pulse. Pennsylvania revealed its quieter charm through scenic waterfalls and peaceful countryside drives.

The East Coast unfolded as a tapestry of history, emotion, and connection: from the grandeur of Washington, D.C., to the nostalgic sweetness of Hershey; from the thunderous power of Niagara Falls to heartfelt visits with family and friends in Vienna, Virginia; from strolling Boston's historic streets and exploring Harvard's iconic campus to celebrating the Fourth of July amid fireworks at Liberty State Park. Monuments and museums: from the Capitol to the Smithsonian, added depth, reminding us how closely history and everyday life intertwine.

Chicago welcomed us with family warmth, world-class museums, and the wonders of the Shedd Aquarium. Orlando became a playground of excitement and adventure, while Miami dazzled with sunlit beaches and vibrant energy. On the West Coast, the rhythm shifted again: Los Angeles stretched wide and restless, Las Vegas shimmered with neon spectacle, and San Francisco charmed us with its fog-kissed Golden Gate.

A week aboard the *MSC Meraviglia* brought a different rhythm altogether. With its nineteen decks and endless horizons, the cruise transformed the sea into both path and destination, gifting us glowing sunrises, lingering sunsets, and memories we will treasure for a lifetime.

Food became a joyful constant throughout the trip, thanks to Neha and Abhishek's thoughtful planning. We savoured flavours from across the globe: American classics and Indian favourites alongside Mexican, Greek, Chinese, Japanese, Thai, Korean, Spanish, Italian, Arabic, and French cuisines. Temples added spiritual grounding and cultural richness, with visits to Balaji Mandir in Chicago and BAPS Akshardham in New Jersey bringing moments of calm reflection. Trekking through Acadia National Park, from Bar Island to scenic viewpoints, allowed us to breathe deeply and reconnect with nature's quiet grandeur.

Movement itself shaped our days: long walks and short drives, buses and ferries, taxis and trams, PATH trains, metros, light rail, and bustling airports alike. Each mode added rhythm to our journey and revealed the country's efficiency and order. Equally memorable were the people we encountered along the way: embassy staff, immigration officers, guides, shopkeepers, and strangers, whose kindness added a human warmth that stayed with us.

Staying with our daughter Neha and son-in-law Abhishek made the journey seamless and deeply joyful. Together, we crossed state lines, shared meals, celebrated milestones, and found happiness in simple moments that became extraordinary. Reuniting with friends and relatives after decades: classmates in Massachusetts, cousins in Chicago and Virginia, and friends in Orlando, San Francisco, and Boston, was profoundly moving. Time may pass, but meaningful connections endure.

As our return to India approached, reality gently resurfaced. Shopping bags multiplied, and soon our luggage did too: two checked-in bags and two cabin bags were no longer enough. With Neha's help, we added an extra bag and prepared carefully for departure. On our final morning, after tea and sandwiches lovingly prepared by her, Neha and Abhishek accompanied us to JFK Airport, helping manage five carefully packed bags.

Check-in went smoothly, and relief washed over us when each suitcase registered exactly twenty-three kilograms. After heartfelt conversations and tearful goodbyes, we cleared immigration and settled into our seats, quietly absorbing the weight of farewell. Even as the plane lifted into the sky, we already missed our beloved daughter and son-in-law, whose care, generosity, and meticulous planning had made every day of our long stay so comfortable and joyous.

Our journey home included a brief stop at Amsterdam's Schiphol Airport before the final flight to Bangalore. Though crowded, the flight allowed us moments of rest and reflection. We landed at eleven that night at Bangalore, adjusted to the nine-and-a-half-hour time difference, collected our luggage, and sent word of our safe arrival to Neha and Abhishek. By one in the morning, we were home, sharing stories with family before sleep finally claimed us.

Looking back, these ninety days were extraordinary: a mosaic of cities and landscapes, culture and cuisine, family and friendship. Coming home brought comfort, yet a part of us still lingers in sunlit avenues, misty mountains, and cheerful ferry rides. Travel teaches us that while the world is vast, it is the connections we form and the experiences we gather that give it meaning.

Returning to India, our hearts were full of gratitude. We realized once again that travel is the finest education: one that teaches humility, connection, and wonder.

"We travel not to escape life, but for life not to escape us."

– Anonymous

APPENDIX: TRIP EXPENSES OVERVIEW

Travel not only enriches the heart but also comes with practical considerations of planning and budgeting.

To offer readers a clear and transparent picture of the preparation behind our ninety-day journey across the United States, the following summary outlines the major expenses incurred during the trip. Actual amounts may vary depending on exchange rates, season, and personal travel choices, but this overview provides a helpful reference for anyone dreaming of a similar adventure.

Category	INR (₹)	USD ($)	Notes
International Airfare (2 pax, round trip)	2,00,000	2,350	Bangalore ↔ USA
Chicago Flights (2 pax, round trip)	44,500	526	Domestic airfare
Miami → New York (post 18-day tour, 2 pax)	22,000	260	Flight, cab, baggage
Extra return baggage to Bangalore	8,500	100	Paid at airport

Category	**INR (₹)**	**USD ($)**	**Notes**
Chariot Tours – 18-Day East & West Coast (2 pax)	12,00,000	14,000	All-inclusive: 4-star hotels, meals, sightseeing, internal flights, ferries, coach travel
MSC Meraviglia Cruise (8 days, 2 pax)	1,35,000	1,600	Cruise fare
Cruise shore excursions (2 pax)	40,500	480	On-shore activities
Cruise service charges & onboard purchases (2 pax)	46,000	540	Tips, drinks, souvenirs
Acadia & Boston – 7-day trip (4 pax)	1,96,000	2,300	Airbnb, hotel, car rental, fuel, food, local expenses
Washington, D.C. bus trip (2 pax)	14,000	168	Round trip
NYC & New Jersey – food, experiences & shopping (3–4 pax)	3,82,000	4,500	Meals, cabs, SIM card, local trips, shopping
Estimated Grand Total	**22,88,500**	**26,824**	All major travel and living expenses

Approximate conversion rate used: ₹85 = USD $1

- **Total (USD): ≈ $26,824**
- **Total (INR): ≈ ₹22,88,500**

Note to Readers

This overview is shared to provide a practical understanding of the scale and planning behind a long-duration international journey. Costs may differ based on travel season, booking timelines, accommodation choices, and individual preferences.

For us, every rupee, every dollar, and every mile contributed to a once-in-a-lifetime experience, one filled with memories far more valuable than numbers on a page.

EPILOGUE: A JOURNEY WITHOUT END

"Wherever you go becomes a part of you somehow."

– Anita Desai

As we look back at our ninety days in the United States, one of the most remarkable realizations is just how vast, diverse, and beautifully preserved the country truly is. Our travels took us across thirteen states, each with its own character, charm, and stories waiting to unfold.

We explored New York City in all its richness; Manhattan's energy, Brooklyn's individuality, Queens' diversity, the quiet corners of Staten Island, the greenery of Bear Mountain, and the thunderous wonder of Niagara Falls. New Jersey became our second home with its calm neighbourhoods: Jersey City, Newark, Hoboken, Bridgewater, Chester, and Edison; setting the rhythm of our daily life.

We stood among monuments in Washington, D.C., absorbed the rhythm of Chicago in Illinois, savoured the sweetness of Pennsylvania, and embraced the sun-filled excitement of Florida: from Orlando's theme parks to Miami's sparkling shores. Massachusetts welcomed us with Boston's history and Worcester's warmth, while Virginia's Ashburn offered peace and hospitality. Maine's Acadia stunned us with its rugged coastline, and California dazzled with the contrasts of Los Angeles and San Francisco.

We took in the majestic landscapes of Arizona: Phoenix and the unforgettable Grand Canyon; as well as the vibrant spectacle of Las Vegas, Nevada. Our cruise added an international glow with the turquoise beauty of the Bahamas.

Along the way, we drove through New Hampshire, Connecticut, Maryland, and Delaware, weaving together a tapestry of landscapes both big and small. Everywhere we went, one truth remained constant: *America's steadfast commitment to nature and environmental care.* Lush gardens, serene lakes, immaculate homes, and beautifully maintained public spaces reflected a culture that values its surroundings deeply.

We were fortunate to visit some of the nation's most extraordinary natural wonders, including the ***Grand Canyon, Acadia, and Everglades***; just three among the 63 national parks. Beyond these, the United States preserves 423 national park system sites, encompassing monuments, memorials, historical landmarks, and heritage areas; many of which enriched our journey.

Among the most cherished memories of our stay were our frequent visits to Lincoln Park in Jersey City. On rainy days or during heatwave warnings, we retreated indoors, enjoying the gym and snooker tables in Neha's building. Misty days hid the New York skyline completely, but on clear nights, we watched the breathtaking view from the terrace: downtown Manhattan glowing golden with each sunset, the bridges gleaming, and even a glimpse of the distant Statue of Liberty.

Nature, too, walked beside us. We spotted foxes, deer, porcupines, hares, skunks, raccoons, capybaras, huge squirrels, and countless birds. Each encounter reminded us of how harmoniously wildlife coexists within the everyday rhythm of American life.

These experiences, big and small, loud and quiet, famous and hidden, shaped the true essence of our journey. They filled our days with wonder, gratitude, and connection.

As we close this chapter of our ninety-day journey, the memories linger like the soft glow of a sunset: warm, vivid, and endless. The shared smiles, the landscapes explored, the quiet mornings and bustling cities, the embraces of family and the kindness of strangers; all have woven themselves into the fabric of our hearts.

No long journey unfolds without its share of uncertainties, and ours, too, reminded us that travel is as much about adaptability as it is about planning. Weather changes, mechanical issues, delays, and diversions are often part of the road. We experienced this firsthand when a cruise we had booked several months in advance was unexpectedly cancelled due to a mechanical fault. Rebooking meant reshaping our itinerary and adjusting carefully planned schedules, but the professionalism and generosity of MSC Cruises, offering reimbursements and discounts, softened the disruption and allowed us to sail at a later, suitable date.

Another moment of uncertainty came during our return journey from Chicago, when our flight was delayed for several hours and eventually diverted. Thankfully, the skies cleared, and we landed safely in Newark. These moments taught us an essential truth of travel: expect the unexpected, embrace flexibility, and trust that every detour carries its own lesson. After all, this, too, is life.

Though the flights have ended and the suitcases unpacked, a part of us remains in every winding trail, glistening skyline, and sun-kissed shore. Travel may have taken us home, but the journey within us continues; an eternal map of love, wonder, and the joy of discovery.

As a veterinarian, I have spent a lifetime caring for life in all its forms; and this journey reminded me that the world itself is a living being: vibrant, beautiful, and deserving of care.

A NOTE OF GRATITUDE: FOR NEHA AND ABHISHEK

This unforgettable journey would not have been possible without the love, dedication, and meticulous planning of our daughter Neha and son-in-law Abhishek. Their guidance shaped every route, every stay, every experience with care and thoughtfulness. From early morning drives to late-night walks on the terrace, from arranging our stays to ensuring our comfort at every step, they transformed our trip into something seamless, joyful, and everlasting. Their affection surrounded us in every city, every meal shared, every laugh enjoyed, and every memory we created together.

This travelogue is not just a record of places: it is a celebration of their love that made our journey smooth, memorable, and evergreen. May this travelogue inspire others to dream, explore, and cherish every step of their own odyssey.

"Journeys may have roads, but memories have no end; they stretch as far as the heart dares."

– Narayan Pratap

ACKNOWLEDGEMENTS

I would like to begin by expressing my deepest gratitude to my mother, Sudha; my brothers, Surya Prakash and Srinivas Manohar; my sisters, Prabha and Priya; and my in-laws, Dr. Ramamohan and Lakshmi, for their constant encouragement, blessings, and love. Their unwavering support has always been my greatest strength.

My heartfelt thanks go to my life partner, Sunitha, whose companionship, patience, and positivity made this entire experience truly joyful and fulfilling.

I am also grateful to the American Embassy for their systematic and efficient visa process, which played a vital role in making this dream journey possible.

A warm thank you to all our relatives and their families whom we met during our stay. Their hospitality, affection, and cherished company will forever remain evergreen in our hearts.

I extend my sincere appreciation to Chariot Travels, Bangalore, for their excellent coordination, and to Mr. Christopher Caress, Cruise Manager of MSC *Meraviglia*, along with his dedicated staff, for ensuring our voyage was truly memorable.

A special note of gratitude to my wonderful college friends, Dr. Thyagaraj, Dr. Paul Chapin, Dr. Shama, and Dr. Gangadhar, and my dear schoolmate, Patanjali, whose company, warmth, and shared excitement made this visit all the more unforgettable.

Finally, my love and appreciation go to our daughter Neha and son-in-law Abhishek, whose enthusiasm, planning, and inspiration brought an extra sparkle to our travels. Their care and dedication transformed this journey into an unforgettable chapter of our lives.

Final Blessing

May every journey awaken your heart to wonder,
every path be lined with kindness,
and every destination leave you wiser, lighter, and grateful.

May the laughter of loved ones accompany your steps,
the beauty of nature and the warmth of strangers enrich your soul,
and each memory shine like a quiet, steady light.

Travel safely, cherish deeply,
and let your heart remain open —
to the surprises, the lessons, and the magic life offers along the way.

CLOSING NOTE TO THE READER

Thank you for taking the time to travel with me through these recollections. What began as a simple desire to record our family holiday gradually transformed into a heartfelt tapestry of moments: places that inspired us, people who welcomed us, and experiences that wove themselves into our memories.

If these pages have brought you a smile, a reflection, or even a spark to explore your own world, then this book has fulfilled its purpose.

May your own travels: near or far, be filled with warmth, harmony, and gratitude.

ABOUT THE AUTHOR

"Across every border and every horizon,
I have found the same truth:
the world is vast, kind,
and worth exploring."

– Dr. Narayan Pratap

Dr. Narayan Pratap is a veterinarian by profession and a traveller by passion. A lifelong learner and explorer, he finds joy in discovering new cultures, experiencing natural wonders, and embracing the warmth of people around the world. His journeys are enriched by the companionship of his wife, Sunitha, whose presence brings joy, meaning, and happy echoes to every adventure.

Over the years, he has visited 21 countries, attending professional training courses, presenting technical papers at conferences, and enjoying memorable family vacations. His travels have taken him across Asia and the Middle East: Malaysia, Singapore, Sri Lanka, Thailand, Oman, and the UAE; as well as Europe: the United Kingdom, France, Germany, Belgium, the Netherlands, Austria, Italy, Vatican City, and Switzerland. Other destinations include Sweden, the Maldives, Indonesia, Canada, Morocco, and most recently, the United States. On many of these adventures, his wife Sunitha and daughter Neha joined him, adding joy, simple delights, and unforgettable family moments.

Each destination has left a unique imprint on their hearts; yet their memorable 90-day expedition across the United States stands out as one of their most cherished experiences. Previously, Dr. Pratap documented their travels across the UK and Europe through a daily Facebook travelogue that was warmly received by friends and well-wishers; their encouragement during his 60-day journey remains deeply appreciated.

Looking ahead, his travel bucket list continues to grow: New Zealand, Australia, Japan, and Vietnam, though, as he likes to say, *"Man proposes, and God disposes."*

When not traveling, Dr. Pratap enjoys writing, photography, and sharing stories that celebrate both the simple and extraordinary moments of life.

This travelogue reflects his belief that "***adventure begins the moment you step out with an open heart, ready to embrace the world in all its wonder.***"